MW00341300

From
GOD

Through
ME

To
YOU

Reflections on My Life
BY PEPPER VON
with Christine Issel

Thank you for all of your love + support...

Pepper Von

ISBN 978-0-9983696-0-0

Printed in the United States of America. Published January 2017
New Frontier Publishing • P.O. Box 6114 • Auburn CA 95604 USA

*This book is dedicated to all those
who are willing to be fearless,
expand their consciousness, to look
at their lives differently, and
find joy every day.*

ACKNOWLEDGMENTS

It is said it takes a village to raise a child:
it takes a community to write a book.
My thanks to every person, place, or thing over the years
that has been part of my journey and
contributed to my being who I am.

I am grateful to all those - past, present, and future -
who allow me to be part of and contribute
to their journey.

For this specific project I'd like to acknowledge
the assistance, cooperation, support, and
encouragement from:
Jackie Anderson, Daniella Bohan, Susan Colbert,
Adrianne Fahey, Stephanie Gates, Kim Goetz,
Keith Goings, Sylvia Gude, Christine Issel,
Greg King, Phyllisann Maguire, Janice Mitchell,
Michael Rainone, Alisa Shubb, Sandy Shubb,
Mary Wright, and the Fierce Funk master trainers.

I would also like to thank
Bishop Sherwood Carthen, Pastor Ron Elmore, and
Reverend Kevin Ross for their mentoring words.
Without all of you this book would not
have come into being.

TABLE OF CONTENTS

Introduction

CHAPTER 1 • Defining Moment 5

CHAPTER 2 • My Backstory 11

CHAPTER 3 • The Civil Rights Movement 33

CHAPTER 4 • Coming of Age 48

CHAPTER 5 • Darkness and Despair 66

CHAPTER 6 • Paths to Success 85

CHAPTER 7 • Life in Sacramento 110

CHAPTER 8 • Building Community 126

CHAPTER 9 • My Lifestyle 146

CHAPTER 10 • Up Close and Personal 163

CHAPTER 11 • Today and Tomorrow 177

Introduction

EVERYONE has a journey and this is mine. It is no better or worse than anyone else's, but it is different and uniquely mine. The opportunities along my path have been exceptional. These are some of the events of my life which show how I became Pepper. You may find there are commonalities with your life so you can relate to parts of my story.

Like everyone else, my life has evolved. To understand the Pepper of today, a certain amount of backstory of my early life is necessary. However, this book is not written in your typical linear fashion. We will meander through my life; you will encounter philosophies known as "Pepperisms," stories, and personal experiences that are not in strict chronological order, nor complete when first mentioned, but become clear as you read further.

My vision is to help unite the world by bringing energies of motivation, non-judgment, inspiration, fun, laughter, health and happiness to the lives of all. For me, this is accomplished by empowering individuals to function within their personal power without fear, so that, in turn, they may live their greatest potential and serve others with love.

I pray before I present, and in the moment, ask Spirit to speak through me. I don't want to say what I want to say; I want to say what those in the audience need to hear. There are times when I will mention situations that were very dark for me or wonderful miracles of salvation. If it is appropriate in the moment and to be shared for reasons I don't need to understand, I simply follow the inspiration, because my words are being choreographed or directed by a Source smarter and more brilliant than I am.

When I am presenting at a convention or running training sessions, the core material and objective of the class doesn't change. However, depending on those present, if the conversation with the students takes a certain turn, and it is relevant to tell a different story in that moment, then I do. I usually share from my life experiences, trusting that God gave me certain experiences in my life through which I made choices—effective or ineffective—to share and use as a teaching tool. There is some flexibility built into what I share. If you give me the same scenario on a different day with a different audience, there's little chance the same experiences will come to the forefront.

People hear what they need to hear. A recent example of this is the comments I received after a presentation at a local university. In the audience were college students, faculty, staff—people who were twenty years older than me and thirty years younger. At the end, some of the students came up with tears in their eyes, saying, "That's exactly what I needed to hear. I don't know how you knew, but you were talking directly to me." One of the older professors came up and said, "That's my walk. I've been there. That's been my shadow. You put me back in touch with my own self and empowered me to continue on my life's journey."

It's a compliment when people share how I've touched their lives, but it is also humbling. It is a gift when this occurs. Even though it has happened many times, I am still shocked and amazed when it does. This feeling of saying the right words is not from a place of ego. I was the vessel for the message—*from* God *through* me.

Through my own experiences I have found when we put more effort and concentration on the outer problem, instead of finding out the corresponding inner problem—and that is always the cause of the outer one—we will have limited success. By the same token, we will get so much more out of all the good things in life—happiness, joy, pleasure—when our soul is healthy. This is when our inner reactions conform to spiritual law.

The energy behind this work is to have us examine our feelings and truths. It is not to have you agree with me. I do not desire to prove you wrong. This implies judgment. There is no good, bad, wrong or right—there is only effective and ineffective at meeting the need to be closer to heaven today than yesterday, and closer tomorrow than today. I don't put any energy in trying to convince you I'm right either. You don't have to be wrong for me to be right. Truth is subjective—it depends on our viewpoint and a given set of parameters at the time.

Pepperisms are about stimulating thinking. Whatever comes up for you as you read through this work is right for you whether or not you agree with me. What you think is absolutely true for you. Again, there is no good, bad, wrong or right—only effective or ineffective. This is not about me.

What is important is how my experiences have played out in my life so that I may share them with you, and through this sharing, support your growth. By using my experiences, I can demonstrate to you that change and growth are not only possible, but are available, and can be yours. Secondly, my sharing lets you know you are not alone, and that I have probably experienced something like what you have been or are presently going through in your life.

Use this work as a guide to help you examine your life and where it takes you in your thoughts, in your life a nd in your actions. The truth you find in what is written may open a new door of understanding for you. Make reading the Pepperisms about you.

I am honored to share my journey with you in anticipation it will help you on your journey through life.

– Pepper Von

CHAPTER 1

A Defining Moment

THROUGHOUT my entire life, my perception of the energies around me has been palpable. I have always had the ability to sense them— on both personal and social levels. This awareness followed me through childhood, as I struggled to grasp and articulate what I was sensing.

While most people are unaware of energies, I have a hyper-awareness. It is not something I can fully explain; it is a spiritual discernment that happens subconsciously. I have simply been able to read energies, the shift in energies, and to respond to them. Growing up, no one else I knew was like me. To this day my siblings talk about how weird I was.

When I had free time my favorite thing to do was to go to the funeral parlor and sit with those who had passed away. I found this fascinating. I would walk in, look at the deceased and their expression, and wonder what their life had been like, what their story was. Oftentimes, I felt the presence, or the energy, of their spirit. Later, this sensing ability would play a big part in a life-defining moment for me.

MARTIAL ARTS

I started studying martial arts when I was seven. The training and experiences I had set the foundation for the mental outlook that has served me throughout my life. I have two black belts, both Korean. I studied Tae Kwon Do which is about kicking and jumping and Tang Soo Do which is based more on using the hands. In the USA, before I joined the Air Force, I did martial arts competitively but not at the professional level.

The early '70s saw the beginning of martial arts competitions, and it became a very popular sport in Japan. It was on Japanese sports television—their version of ESPN and had famous sponsors such as Kodak, Yamaha and Suzuki. Martial arts was not the most favorite national sport, but it was a popular sport with many followers. When people found out there was an American team, Team USA, it was a big deal that Americans were competing.

In 1978, during my early twenties, I was in the Air Force stationed in Tokyo, Japan. As I increased my skills in martial arts, I started kick-boxing there, and was televised on the professional competitive level as a member of the American international kickboxing team—Team USA.

Kickboxing, as a hybrid martial art, originated in Japan in the 1960s and eventually became known as Mixed Martial Arts (MMA). MMA is a combat sport involving a variety of disciplines like jiu-jitsu, judo, karate, boxing and wrestling—usually a combination of all these. Competitors strike using hands, feet, knees, or elbows. You grapple for submission, using chokeholds, throws, or takedowns so that your opponent taps out, hitting the mat to let the referee know he gives up. Technically we weren't allowed to grapple—to throw each other to the floor and wrestle. There was either light or no contact. Scoring was on a point system. You received points for not striking what could have been a deathblow, demonstrating what you could have done but chose to control instead. Muay Thai, the style I competed in, was considered the ultimate contact form of kickboxing.

Competing as a martial arts fighter in the welterweight class was outside my military duty. My trainers in regular martial arts, who were also in the military, encouraged me to get involved in mixed martial arts at the professional level. I wasn't paid much to compete, even though there were contracts. Competing didn't pay like it does currently where you become famous and can buy a house on the hill. Today fighters can travel within their own country and all over the world to compete in matches, and they become celebrities.

As a member of Team USA, I had a responsibility and financial agreement with the team. But since I was in the military at the time, it was like having a second job. Being in the military also prevented me from entering into any ironclad contracts. The Air Force was my first responsibility and there was always the possibility of being shipped out, so there was some flexibility in my contract. If I had to leave the team, someone would step in and take my place.

I didn't need a sponsor. Being a sponsor meant paying for some of the fighter's training in exchange for him wearing T-shirts and shorts with the logo advertising your business. There weren't any promotional tours or appearances either. However, another activity I was doing at the time was performing in a "Soul Train" production. If I was doing interviews for the show, my competing in kickboxing always came up and I was able to promote mixed martial arts competitions in that way.

You had to have an 80% win record as an individual to be invited to join Team USA. There were four of us who fought for Team USA, not counting what in basketball would be called the bench. I fought ten champion level fights for Team USA.

I was part of a training team—we weren't all in the Air Force. Some team members came from the States but were living and working in Japan, yet nearly every kickboxing fighter had studied martial arts as a lifelong vocation. We trained in different dojo locations around Tokyo. My training schedule worked around my job as a medic, and the team championship fights were scheduled well in advance.

Training takes major dedication. Experienced fighters are in top shape. There were weeks or months between fights when all you did was train. I was training about four hours a day—either all at once or broken up into two sessions. The focus was on endurance training. There was a lot of running, a lot of rope work, a lot of kicking—pounding your body to be prepared to get pounded. I was bruised a lot after a fight. There was a lot of sparring and not much weight training. There were no dietary restrictions—the only reason you dieted in those years was to make your weight class. You didn't eat fries and milk shakes if it was going to take you from welterweight to middleweight.

Today, tattoos and shaved heads are popular with fighters— not back then. Many had nicknames, but I was simply known as Pepper. We would showboat when entering the arena showing off how fast and flashy our kicks were, or how fast our hands were. I didn't do trash talking or anything flashy. That just wasn't my style. Besides it didn't matter, because my opponents didn't speak English.

Kickboxing is as much a cerebral competition as it is physical. You must think fast under pressure to outwit your opponent. In the ring, if you take your eyes off your opponent to flinch, you can't see where the next punch or kick is coming from. And any good fighter will take immediate advantage of your loss of focus. It's an intense sport, when the fight changes, you have to adjust. You must stay focused and cool emotionally; otherwise you'll lose. Though serious injuries were rare, they did happen.

DEATH IN THE RING

FIGHTS seem different on TV: less violent. It's a charged atmosphere in the arena: the music, the lights, the cheering. Everyone is hyped; the energy is electric. We fought in a regular boxing or wrestling ring without a cage. After we fought, we never left ringside because we could be called in as a substitute for someone else on the team who was injured and taken out. The night the incident happened I had already fought.

The roar of the audience almost drowned out the hard rock music blaring throughout the event center. Suddenly one of the fighters went down and the referee stopped the fight. Immediately the doctor was in the ring and people were running in with lung inflators, towels, neck stabilizers and stretchers. It wasn't like in the U.S. when someone gets hurt in a football game and the crowd goes quiet waiting for the emergency crew to come out with its equipment, and hopefully the athlete limps off the field. No one went quiet. The crowd kept cheering!

I knew the Japanese fighter from the circuit, but not personally. Within a short time the doctor pronounced the fighter dead. At that moment, I paid no attention to the audience. While people were cheering all around the entire arena, the cheers of the crowd faded from my mind; I didn't feel the heat from the lights or hear the music. I was in a different zone. The only conscious thought I had was an absolute focus on the mood of the moment. My experience with reading energy was suddenly reawakened.

I was conscious on two planes—the physical and the energy plane. My mind was crisp and clear. There were no stray thoughts or information coming or going out of my mind. My inner voice was crisp—my state of consciousness became multi-dimensional. My thoughts became centered again on the energy I was feeling.

A light bulb went on for me about how barbaric the sport could be. Somewhere I'd lost the fact that competition kickboxing was life-threatening. In my mind, I had glamorized it by thinking I was a professional athlete, and this was my sport. As a sports competitor, I accepted there were certain risks. In my mind's eye, the risk is low and being good or the best at the sport is what I focused on in a fight. The risk of death was so far removed from my brain. Every single one of us on the team had falsely accepted that a serious injury or accident would never happen to us.

Satisfaction in conquering a worthy challenger was what drove me. Then in a moment of clarity where there was a loss of life, it was clear to me that this was the potential of every single fight. I realized I had gotten caught up in the artificial and hyped atmosphere of the sport.

To be present at the time of tragedy was not like reading about it or seeing it on TV or in the movies. It was clear to me: I could be one or two fights away from being that fighter on the canvas. The odds were against me, and if a three-minute round could have been six minutes earlier, that fighter could have been me.

As I looked around, the cheering energy of the crowd and the drama in the ring didn't match. The loss and seriousness of the tragedy that was going on in the ring and the celebration of the crowd was too much of a contrast and resulted in an awakening in me.

This was the first signal that competing was not the reason I had studied martial arts. I was a natural-born fighter, fighting as a sport, not as a way of bullying others. I had gone into it for a love of movement and fitness, of perfecting something—the forms and the movement of the hands. To me, katas, the sequence of movements in martial arts, is like a dance. Now they allow katas to music in competition. Back then they didn't. Everything was about precision. For me it was about the craft, not self-defense. When I was younger I wanted to become accomplished as a martial artist, not as a fighter. For me, martial arts was about getting centered and developing self-confidence. It was about gaining control of my emotions.

The fallout I witnessed cut through my consciousness when I heard the crowd cheering but saw a mother, a girlfriend and other members of the family crying. I saw the tragedy at that point and what was really at risk. Abruptly, there was not a lot standing between my reality and the possibility of death.

The conflict in energy between the cheering crowd and the suffering family was disturbing to me. I saw the emotional loss to his family. The real pain of loss made the dangers of competition clear to me. You can lose a match and get another match, but for this fighter it was his last. He wouldn't get a second chance. This was a real loss; this fighter would never fight again.

At 23, I didn't like what I saw, experienced and felt. I understood I was never born to be the person I had become. I realized I had gotten caught up on the wrong side of a runaway train. According to the system of this sport, I hadn't done anything wrong. In that system you're praised if you win. But in my personal value system, I was off-track. It took this unfortunate incident as a way for me to stop and evaluate what I was doing. Even in that moment, what was being juggled back and forth in me was the pain I saw in the family and the thought it could have just as easily been me. In my case that realization didn't sit well. To me, in that instance, I knew this was not what I wanted to do. In that second, kickboxing was no longer a sport.

Suddenly for me, Tokyo was a long way from my roots in Clarksdale, Mississippi and a million miles away from my upbringing and who I was. I resigned from the team immediately. When I made the decision to quit, I had a contract that I fulfilled for one more individual fight and never fought after that.

CHAPTER 2

My Backstory

LIFE is a crazy quilt of experiences, each represented by small pieces of cloth stitched together to form a bigger piece of fabric that forms the background of daily life. As everyone does, I have qualities in my nature that are shaped by the choices I've made in my past. But the fabric of my life, as with most people, begins with the contributions of my parents and grandparents.

MY FATHER'S FAMILY

MY granddad on my father's side, Clay Von, Sr., served in the Army in World War II. He joined early in the war effort when he was in his 30s. The many American black GIs who returned from WWII found little opportunities for employment in the Delta region of Mississippi as segregation and discrimination continued. My granddad was retired by the time I was old enough to know him.

My father's mother's name was Mary. We called her Grandmama. She was short, with medium brown skin, and was a little on the stockier side, but not obese. She owned a café. My father only had one sister, Elizabeth, who we called Aunt Liz.

Grandmama's 4th Street Café was a popular landmark, and in the heart of our part of town it was a meeting place. There were no shopping malls, and 4th street was the center of our world. You went to 4th Street for everything you needed and to socialize. It was where the bars, restaurants, beauty and barbershops, and other businesses were located. It was the main street connecting our neighborhood within black Clarksdale and lead straight to downtown and then into Clarksdale's white neighborhood.

Grandmama's café was open for breakfast, lunch and dinner so she had long days. Like most of the little juke joints—little one-room cafés where food and liquor were sold—Grandmama had a jukebox that played music on a coin-operated machine where customers could choose what they wanted to hear. In the café the jukebox played blues and a selection of gospel music—especially Mahalia Jackson. Playing Mahalia Jackson kept Grandmama connected spiritually throughout her week or anytime she needed the uplifting her faith brought her. Of course, I grew up listening to gospel music.

Both my parents are natives of the Clarksdale area. My father, Clay Von, Jr., also served in the Navy in WWII. He joined right out of high school. Physically, my dad had an average body build for someone 5'5". My father looked just like his father—same height, same build, same face and same complexion. If you progress the aging process in my father, they look exactly the same at the same age.

My dad was a blues drummer, singer, comedian and emcee in the group CV Veal and the Shufflers—shufflers as in dancers. Monk—as in monkey—was his name in the blues band and his nickname. To this day his friends call him Monk, not CV. He was a fiery entertainer—he'd dance, be all over the place, jump on the counter and start singing. He was known for his sense of humor. He was a natural comedian.

I think very highly of my dad. He shaped my values. I saw him become an awesome man of God. He takes life as it comes, stays humble, healthy and happy. I admire him for a couple of characteristics. One is his amazing sense of humor. He finds laughter somewhere every day in the rollercoaster of life with its twists and turns. I also admire his ability to stay calm in dealing with life circumstances, his management of emotions and remaining true to his passion for music. I only saw him deal with or accept things in life fully. There is no almost or maybe or somewhat with him—he is always fully committed. Traits that are hard or harder to find in people today, he has.

My dad was always a musician, but he also held other jobs, so we had food and clothes and everything we needed. He worked as a supermarket manager and did janitorial services for big retail stores. He did pick-up and delivery for the dry cleaners. Just like today, artists or people in entertainment wait tables or may have two or three jobs to pay the bills, but their art is their lifework and their passion. To be a fully committed musician or artist, it is hard to hold down a 9-5 job, but you do that so you can follow your passion.

Over the 1940s and '50s, a blending of the music of white back-country balladeers with black rhythm and blues had been evolving. Clarksdale's contribution to the world of blues, R&B and soul is historically significant. It is the home of the Delta Blues Museum and is designated as part of the Mississippi Blues Trail by the Mississippi Blues Commission in recognition of its importance in the development of the blues in Mississippi. Plaques in downtown Clarksdale commemorating musicians include one honoring my dad. There's one for Ike Turner, and one for Sam Cooke who became a well-known R&B, soul, gospel, pop, jazz, singer-songwriter and entrepreneur. Ike Turner has frequently been referred to as a "great innovator" of rock and roll by his contemporaries Little Richard and Johnny Otis. Phil Alexander, once editor-in-chief of Mojo magazine, described Turner as "the cornerstone of modern day rock 'n' roll". He was my second cousin on my dad's side.

My dad played with the likes of B. B. King, Ike Turner, James Johnson and other hardcore blues musicians. He was a drummer in Turner's Kings of Rhythm band. With Clarksdale vocalist Jackie Brenston, Turner's band, billed as the Delta Cats, recorded "Rocket '88," the song many consider to be the first rock 'n' roll record, at Sam Phillips' studio in Memphis in 1951—three years before Elvis Presley began his recording career at the same studio and four years before I was born. I didn't see Turner very often. By the late '50s, Ike had begun making a name for himself and had left Clarksdale.

When my father played, he mostly played in juke joints. Everything happened in that one room. He performed all the time—he was never not performing. Wherever he performed on Friday nights, I couldn't go because I was too young to be in a juke joint. But when his band played any open show, like an outdoor performance, I went to see him.

Being in Clarksdale, where blues is so prevalent and musical instruments were available to me, I learned to play early. Before my parents separated, the band rehearsed at our house and my dad's drums were sitting around the house all the time. It was only natural the first instrument I learned to play was the drums and later the guitar. Initially, I played by ear.

It was in junior high when I was playing in the school band that I began to take lessons. Clifton Morris was the music teacher, and our families were close. He had two daughters around my age, and his wife was one of my elementary school teachers. Mr. Morris was the bass player in my dad's band. I learned to read music and to play the bass and guitar from him. His ear for the bass line of music, like my dad's ear for percussion and rhythm, was excellent, and he was a big influence on me.

Our Catholic school was too small to have a band class, but we had a school band that played for Mass and other events. It was a combo band as opposed to a marching band. We didn't have a piano in my house, but I played one at school. My mother's sister, Aunt Saint, whose house in Ohio my sister and I went to every summer for a couple of months, had a piano. I took lessons there. I would sit for hours and hours and play. At school I was in choir. At our Baptist church, I was in the choir and was the director of the children's choir.

Musically, my favorite artist, and the one who has influenced me the most artistically, is my father. Without bias, he's one of the best blues drummers I've ever seen or heard.

Although my parents didn't live together, my dad still had a huge influence and presence in my life. His contributions were not so much what he said as the way he lived life and got things done, the way he resolved situations. My calm, my logic, my ability to communicate with people and my actions come from my dad. He didn't verbalize any of these traits. I saw them in how he acted in our family, in work situations, how he handled life situations, and how he handled my life situations as I was growing up. He was the peacekeeper. There was strength in his gentleness. His method was always, "Let's do it the way it should be done first and see how that plays out."

When I visit Mississippi, I reconnect with the sense that my father's needs are basic and his joys in life are simple pleasures. Seeing the way he enjoyed a life that was creatively chaotic, but not destructively chaotic, is inspiring. Using music as a metaphor, as with any kind of creative expression and especially when you are performing, you learn to go with the flow. There are times you pick up the pace, and there are times you slow down a bit. Sometimes you play a little differently than you normally would. My dad applied that to life. Whatever he was doing, my dad was always calm and patient. My mom, on the other hand, wasn't the queen of calm and patience—she was a drama queen.

The way my father valued chivalry inspired me, too. I saw him practice that with every female in our lives. It didn't matter if he was arguing with my mom—chivalry was never absent. The way he interacted with my sisters, my grandmothers, other women in our community, at church or at the store, it didn't matter—he was very respectful. That was an important value to him. My dad was not a physically violent person, even though he boxed while in the Navy; in domestic spats, he always treated my mom with respect. One of the things both my parents did was to show respect to older people no matter what their character or how abrasive their personality was.

I grew up at a time when society was at a crossroads of making a transition as far as teenagers were concerned – when it became okay to talk back to your parents and there was more physical aggression. I remember my dad saying to me, "If I ever hear of you being disrespectful to your mother or your sisters, or hitting them," which to me translated to any female, "there would not be a place on this earth you could hide from me." This wasn't a threat of violence, it was about him expressing his feeling and making his point clear. He left the outcome open—he didn't express what the ramification would be, only that there would be consequences.

At the time we were all living with Mama, my maternal grandmother, my parents had lots of spats. I believe most of their domestic disputes were alcohol induced. They were so loud. The sound felt to me like it was amplified. I'd cover my ears with a pillow. I couldn't go to a part of the house and cover my ears well enough to not hear them. Being in the living room I remember putting pillows over my ears, and I could not escape the noise. I didn't care if they kept shouting; I just didn't want to hear it. I felt angry because I couldn't not hear it, and that's all I wanted to do.

MY MOTHER'S FAMILY

MY mother's mother was Idella Topps, known to the family and close friends as Libay. In my younger years, we all lived together in a multi-generational family. We lived in her house that was a two-bedroom, one-bath, typical post-WWII house. Most of the houses in our neighborhood had a shotgun floor plan—you could open the front door and see through to the back door. Later when I was in junior high, my parents bought a mobile home that sat in my grandmother's yard.

We were not literally raised by our grandmother, but our grandmother was as much in our life as our mother was. Because she lived in the same household, she shared parenting duties. Libay was called "Mama" by my mother, and that's what we called her too. Everyone called my mother by her name or her nickname, so I also called my mother by her first name. My cousins did the same thing—calling their mothers by their first names—especially if they were raised in the same household with their grandmother.

On my mother's side there was more "white blood" so Mama was taller, slim and very light-skinned. My mother's sisters were light-skinned too. My mother had two sisters and two brothers. My grandfather on my mother's side I didn't know at all. He and my grandmother were already separated when I was born and he lived in Detroit. Mama worked at White Rose Dry Cleaners as a seamstress and presser. It was located on 4th Street across the street from my other grandmama's café.

My mother was Marian. That's a family name for both males and females, with many family members over the years sharing that name. Tootie was what everyone called her.

My mother was the darkest skinned of her siblings. She took more after her father. She was small, about the same height or a little shorter than my father. Average build and on the thinner side, she was the smallest of all her siblings, and she became crippled as a child. One leg was extremely shorter than the other. This eventually caused hip dysplasia, arthritis and everything that came with it. She always smoked and had emphysema that eventually became lung cancer. It is hard for me to remember when she wasn't sick. She was really thin when she was sick.

Tootie was educated in the Clarksdale public elementary schools, graduated from Coahoma Agricultural High School and Coahoma Junior College. She owned a beauty salon, but was also a school teacher. She was employed for nearly 30 years at Coahoma Opportunities, Inc., working in the Head Start program. My dad was in his 30s when they married. I was born on Tootie's 32nd birthday.

People liked Tootie because she was always being of service. She inspired many people with her friendly, kind and patient ways. She had so much patience for others. She would always make herself available for church or neighborhood projects. However, what I saw and experienced at home was very different. She would come home tired, right before she went out drinking or when she came in from drinking. I didn't see the patient and kind side of her very often. At home she was naturally short-tempered and dramatic. We lived on eggshells. The alcohol shortened her fuse. Perhaps some of that came from harboring her own angry emotions of being the darkest skinned, when in those days that was not good. Or it could have come from the limp she had most of her life.

My musical ability and performing, along with my centeredness, comes from my dad. I am most like him. He is a strong, gentle person—a thinker—and uses logic rather than emotions. Because of these traits, he appears passive. My mother, on the other hand, had this aggressive energy about her. She could be loud, intimidating and swear like a sailor. I just remember her yelling and screaming and being angry a lot. My mother's influence contributed to my stubbornness, a trait I shared with her. It was her way or no way, and she was willing to fight to the death for her beliefs. We lived with her in a house with all the alcohol-induced problems that come with that lifestyle. From her behavior, I refused to ever drink, and I avoid conflict at any cost, sometimes to my detriment.

I became a "parent pleaser," because she was always upset. I am someone who avoids conflict, so I would always do whatever kept her calm. That shaped a lot of how I function under duress and pressure, not wanting to tell people "no" or to draw boundaries, because I don't want them to be upset. I became an overachiever so she would always be proud of me. She was physical in her discipline. Back in those days, the rule was "spare the rod; spoil the child." Whatever she was closest to she would throw, and if she wasn't close to anything she'd take her shoe off.

THE ONLY WAY OUT IS ALL THE WAY IN

WHEN we are busy pleasing everyone, we are not being true to ourselves and trying to please others is an assured path to stress and failures in life.

PLEASING OTHERS

DO I have a fear of not living up to the expectations of others? Am I more motivated by the fear of failure? That's how I used to work. As a youngster, I was taught to please, or learned to please. I've always been a pleaser, even to my own detriment—even if I was angry, abused or hurt, it didn't matter how much I suffered.

It was easy for me to become an habitual—it became my addiction. The drug is making sure you win over others so they are happy with you. The same feeling can also make it so you don't try if you don't think you can live up to the expectations of others or the new bar you have set by your own past successes. Growing up, I didn't recognize or understand the psychology behind my behavior as I do now.

When I was young my parents would say, "Oh, he's so talented; he's a good kid." I would get the praise I always wanted. As a teen, I was on all these committees at school. I was the class president. I had a job after school and I was playing an instrument. I never got in trouble. All of these activities were things I wanted to do, but more important-ly they were ways of gaining my hidden agenda of pleasing others, making them happy and loving me. Pleasing others was my learned behavior. Unconsciously I knew that it brought me the big payoffs I sought—praise, acceptance and love.

Pleasing others still contributes to my character and paints some of the way I function today, but I've modified it. I am sure that a rem-nant of that behavior is part of being a pleaser when I ask myself: Why would I settle for mediocrity in anything I do? If it is going to be worth the investment of my interest, time, resources and emotions, then it's worth doing all the way in.

Reflecting back on my life, the motto of "the only way out is all the way in" started when I was seven years old and began studying martial arts. Why would I not go for a black belt? That was the ultimate level. There are all these colored belts along the way where I could have stopped and said: "Hey, I'm pretty good, I'm cool". For some reason, I was propelled to always take things to the extreme. For me, it was a black belt two times over! If I am going to play an instrument, why not play five? Why not be able to orchestrate the whole song by myself? If I was going to do aerobics, why not be the national champion?

The phrase of "the only way out is all the way in" has currently taken on a different meaning for me. The way I define it in my life now is that "all the way in" means doing my very best, maximizing my potential whatever that is. So instead of meaning I have to be the champion so everyone praises me, I do it for me. Now it means if I'm going to make the commitment, I require I do my absolute best. I still set my standards higher than most, but doing one's best is all we can ask of ourselves or others.

For some, people pleasing comes with the feeling of dreading to say yes, but feeling powerless to say no. Then there's the guilt that comes along with saying no: "I'm a bad person if I say no." The question we should stop and ask before we say yes is: "What effect will making this obligation have on me?" We need to consider the effects an obligation will have on our time, on our mental, physical, spiritual, and emotional selves, and the commitments we've already made to others.

If what's being asked of us is something we have said yes to before, but in our heart and mind we were saying, "I hate this…," and the situation has come around again, we now have the opportunity to be honest and say no. No is a complete sentence. We don't have to justify saying no. When we choose to say yes, then we are honor-bound to follow through with our word, doing our maximum best. Being the best we can be is a lifelong endeavor.

All parents are imperfect. They are literally not taught how to express their love for a child or a person based on the other person's needs. Tootie loved us the best and only way she knew how. As a result, I found my own way to exist in the household with her energy.

As an adult, my survival mechanism is the result of how I learned to function as a child. My initial self-discipline was from fear. There were times I did what I did because I didn't want to die. As I grew, my self-discipline was based on respect for my own values and my need to control myself.

Being of service to other people is the trait I get from Tootie. Not that my father didn't help others, but she was well known for helping other people through hard times. She was always organizing many of the church projects and fundraisers. As an example, she set up a program for feeding the hungry. If someone's house burned down, she organized benefits to help them. She organized making food baskets for the needy at Thanksgiving and Christmas. She was a talented crafts person and was recognized in the community for her sewing, quilting, arts and crafts. She was a very compassionate and physically giving person. She may not have been emotionally giving, but she gave to those in need.

I have an older sister, Saint Marian. Saint Marian's pet name was Chic—pronounced Chick. She is only a year older than I am. When we were growing up there was no such thing as "latchkey kids" (kids who come home to an unsupervised house). You don't hear that term too much anymore because it's become the norm rather than the exception. Back in the day when I was a kid, it was the exception. Whether your parents were home or not, you knew you were supposed to go directly home from school and do your chores.

When we were both too young to be at home without it being dangerous, we went to our neighbor's house—the lady right next door. As we got older, we went to our parents' shops or place of business. As soon as possible, I started working at the Pride Supermarket with my dad. Pride Supermarket was the first black-owned, big supermarket in town. Today, it would be a smaller version of Safeway. It sold mostly groceries.

God gave me grandmothers with good Southern words of wisdom to which I listened. We didn't sit down and have philosophical discussions—it was just how things they said came up in everyday life. Like many parents, both black and white of that era, my grandparents told me one thing, over and over: "Love God, be a good person, be good to people." Mama always said over and over, "Leave a place better for you having been there than it was when you got there."

You always went to your grandparents when your parents didn't give you what you wanted. Your grandparents were the stable ones who had lived through more of life's experiences, so they had more wisdom on which to base advice. Both played their grandmother role completely. With age, they had a softer, more nurturing side. However, they were disciplinarians in that they were strict and consistent about not letting us get into trouble.

GRATITUDE

MY grandmother Mary always said, "Wherever you end up, remember you didn't get there by yourself. You owe a lot of people gratitude." In our day-to-day struggles we often forget this; we think we did it all by ourselves. We forget the contributions of our second-grade teacher. Gratitude keeps you humble and connected. As great as you are, your greatness is a compilation of contributions by a lot of people. This attitude also suggests that your responsibility is to gratefully acknowledge their contribution, because that's how you became who you are.

MY OWN FAMILY

I was born Billy Von Veal. Chic is not really my sister. Her birth mother is my mom's sister, who wasn't around. We grew up together since we were babies. A lot of us cousins grew up together. Chic and I were together every day. We went to the same school, the same church. Even though my mother was present in the household, we were literally raised together by our grandmother. We were pre-teens before we knew we weren't actually brother and sister, but cousins. Yet all of our lives we've been referred to as brother and sister. Even our family members refer to us that way. My blood sister is eight years younger than I am. Her name is Marian Yvonne, and her nickname is Dot. As we grew up, the girls held on to their nicknames.

My family and school friends always called me by my full name, Billy Von Veal, pronouncing it as one word, "Billyvonveal." My nickname when I was young, from people old enough to be my great-grandparents, was Bubba. I got the name Pepper while in high school because I was a "hot" martial arts fighter. My best friend was Tyronne, known as Ty. We were in high school together, went into the military together. We called each other brothers even though we weren't blood related.

I live in the present not the past. I'm the type of person who focuses on what I am supposed to be doing right now. Therefore, I don't remember much about my childhood. The first memories I have are of band practices at the house with dad and his friends, and my mom and grandmother having meetings of the church women there. I remember visiting my aunt in Ohio and different aunts in Chicago and St. Louis during school vacations.

One thing I do remember is that when I was around seven I wanted to take martial arts classes. My mother said she wasn't going to run us all over town to different lessons; what one did, the other did. Chic wanted to take a tap dance class. I accompanied her to dance class, and she took karate class with me. This began my lifelong love affair with dance. I like movement and grew up taking tap, jazz dance, and ballet along with karate. I eventually earned two black belts in martial arts. Aside from karate and dance, I played baseball and basketball in school, because we had a small school and everybody got to play everything. I played because I liked being busy and thought it was fun. My mom said I'd always been a busy kid. She said, "If you didn't have five things going on at once, you were a mess." I've always had artistic and creative A.D.D.

GROWING UP IN THE SOUTH

CLARKSDALE is a city in the Mississippi Delta region, the western county boundary being the Mississippi River itself. It is an agricultural and trading center as well as the county seat of Coahoma County. When I was young, Clarksdale was identified by the big water tower or the cotton gin on Highway 61. Whenever you were going out or coming into Clarksdale, you knew you were home when you passed the cotton gin.

Clarksdale was small enough to retain its Southern character where people knew you and who your people were. In spite of its smaller size, Clarksdale's inner city neighborhoods were no stranger to poverty, drugs, crime, street thugs, racial prejudice and segregation. There were lots of ways to get into trouble if you wanted to.

Although I had been to Chicago and St. Louis, as I was growing up I didn't know much about other places. For example, I didn't know Memphis, just a few miles up the road, was considered a bigger city. Population-wise Clarksdale was considered a small city. As of the 2010 census, the population of Clarksdale was 26,151, with a racial makeup of the city being 75.5% black and 22.9% white.

Clarksdale wasn't like Mayberry (of The Andy Griffith Show), but it wasn't Chicago either. It was big enough to have things to do. There were activities going on in city schools, and there was a downtown community center with wrestling matches to attend.

I never felt like I lived in a small town because some of my relatives lived in the rural area around Clarksdale. Much of my rearing was out in the country where my parents were born. We would often be out there visiting relatives, so in comparison, I always felt like I lived in the city.

There was no integration in Clarksdale in the '50s and '60s; there was a white section and a black section. In my neighborhood, we saw a few whites, perhaps the owners of little corner food stores, a student teacher who came from another state, or the Catholic nuns, but they all lived outside of the neighborhood. We didn't have white neighbors. Even though I went to Catholic school with white nuns and white priests, the student population was black.

I think my parents chose to send me to Catholic school to keep me more engaged in a spiritual element—something Christian-based, rather than the secular public school. I went to public school several years until there was an opening for me in the Catholic school in the third grade.

When most students started Catholic school in kindergarten they stayed all the way through high school, so I had to wait for an opening. The public schools had more students, but there was more discipline in Catholic schools. Both schools were within walking distance in my neighborhood.

In school I was involved in Catholic activities; I was even an altar boy and played in the church band. But we also had our own black churches. We belonged to the Chapel Hill Missionary Baptist church, a Southern Baptist church, where I was baptized and where I was involved in activities too.

Growing up, my world was small enough that my life revolved around the culture of Clarksdale and my immediate neighborhood. Adults were always accessible to us, even if they were at work. More often than not, we were engaged in what they did. When my parents went to work, I would walk to where they were after school—I worked in the store with my father. Or I would walk from school to my grand-mother's café and worked with her. Down the street was the dry clean-er where my other grandmother worked. As we got older, after school we'd go there and press clothes. Across the street was the beauty salon my mother owned. It wasn't all work and no play because I was so involved in outside activities.

It was the '60s, the time of the civil rights era. You could feel the energy of change, and Clarksdale was at the center of that change. Yet the village mentality of family was still strong. You knew you couldn't go down the street and do something wrong, because it seemed like before you were out of the house and down the street your parents already knew or would find out about what you did. Neighbors could discipline you. In general, there was a lot more respect overall.

As kids, we'd run in and out of each other's houses with no consideration to knocking on doors or asking permission, even if the neighbors didn't have kids. You could run in and get a glass of Kool Aid or a glass of water and run back out into the street to play. Everyone knew you and you were safe.

There was the attitude that it takes a village to raise a child. People didn't have a problem with discipline coming from other non-related adults. There was a commitment to education, to self-respect. There were rules. You didn't curse if you were having a hard time or stubbed your toe. Let alone ever hear it on the radio. You didn't swear in front of or behind your parents' backs, or within the hearing of anybody— whether your parents were there or not. You didn't hit your sister. My father would say, "I don't care what they did. It isn't okay to hit girls."

There were boundaries. If the streetlights were about to come on, you better not be in the street playing. You better be home. We struggled to meet those boundaries. We'd play to the last second and be running down the street to be home before dark. If your mom stood on the front porch and called your name, it would echo three blocks down. You didn't have to wonder if it was your mom or if she was talking to you—you knew. There was no doubt. If you responded back, "I'll be there as soon as I finish…," that wasn't acceptable. These were all components of life in the city that kept you grounded and provided you with security.

MY PARENTS' SEPARATION

ONE day my dad left for the last time. Before that he would leave and come back; but on that day he left to cool off and he got in the car with way too many of his belongings. In my gut – which I have always been connected to, even though I couldn't understand it at the time – I knew he was leaving for good. My parents separated shortly after my sister Dot was born and I was around eight. They led separate lives for 50 years but they were never officially divorced. Until the day she passed, over 40 years later, my mother wore her wedding ring and considered my dad her best friend. To this day my dad still wears his wedding ring.

I think at the time it was their lifestyle with the alcohol, the blues band, the traveling, and juke joints that contributed to the separation. When they were both drinking—I think he drank less than she did—it was still hard to manage everything and be a parent too.

At eight it's hard for kids to realize their parents splitting up has nothing to do with them, that they didn't do anything wrong, and it's not that they aren't loved. Because Mama was living next door to us, the split wasn't as disruptive as it could have been. We didn't have to change schools or places to live. Some grandparents, like mine, were the cohesive element in black families. My maternal grandmother, Mama, being such an integral part of our life, really helped raise us right. Otherwise we could have gotten into trouble. Both grandmothers made sure we attended church and school.

In my family, there were elements of inspiration, too. There was always music, there was culture—our own black culture—and a pride in that culture. Activities were available for you to stay connected to this culture. There were educational institutions, there were activities to remind you to keep going, keep getting better, keep learning, continuing to thrive by latching on to something; whether it was music or poetry, it didn't matter. I never heard in my house, or in my family, or in the neighborhood, that you couldn't do something, that there were things out of my reach, or my range of possibility. There was always a lot of encouragement. All those elements made Clarksdale valuable to me. I saw people who looked like me who owned their own businesses. It didn't matter if it was a barbershop, or a beauty salon, or shoeshine stand. We could see the pride of ownership within the neighborhood. We also learned some element of cross-cultural acceptance. Many of the neighborhood businesses—for example, the convenience stores on the corner—were owned by other ethnic races. There was some cultural interaction in the neighborhood but not in the city at large.

I was also raised in a neighborhood that I understand now was poor. But back then we had no idea; everybody else was the same. We had secondhand shoes and clothes. To go buy secondhand shoes for Easter was a big treat. We had to go to the "white side" of town to see any socio-economic differences.

My folks both worked, so we weren't the poorest of the poor at that time, even though we had food that was stamped "government cheese," "government powdered milk." The reason you had food in your pantry was because your mom or grandmother made and canned preserves in the summertime. You didn't just run out and buy canned peaches. Everyone had a garden in the backyard; you learned how to grow vegetables. We didn't have skin lotion. You used Royal Crown hair grease or Vaseline Petroleum Jelly and yes, even Crisco. There was not a lot of need for things that we, today, think we need just to survive.

YOUTHFUL ENTERTAINMENT

WHEN you don't have money, you use your environment to play and find entertainment. We found ways to challenge and entertain ourselves, to occupy our time. We looked for simple fun that didn't cost money. In those days, kids took a stick and drew in the dirt, built forts, made mud pies. We even used sticks to hit beehives or chase snakes under the house. That was, for the most part, what we did. That was boy fun—it was us being naïve, young, and having fun that didn't acknowledge danger. Exploring and using our environment was okay as long as it didn't hurt yourself or anyone else.

The Sunflower River ran through our city. It is a distant offshoot of the Mississippi. We considered it a river, but compared to the wide Mississippi it was a ditch. Still, it was classified as a river. The Sunflower River begins above Clarksdale and flows directly south 100 miles to join the larger Yazoo River before dumping into the Mississippi. The Sunflower is heavily silt-laden with mud from the bayou and smaller streams that feed into it. It has mucky brown water with floating debris, plus snakes and everything else found in any Mississippi waterway.

There were big pipes running across the Sunflower. I am not sure if they were sewer or water pipes, but the pipes ran across from one bank to the other. They were very narrow pipes and if you wanted to walk on them you had to balance and walk as if you were walking a tightrope. At 12, for fun, with the sun shining down on us, my cousin Michael and Tyronne and I would balance and walk out, one foot in front of the other, to stand in the middle of the river. There was no land directly under us, and the river flowed fast. We carried rocks and threw them at the snakes.

Another time, my sister Chic and I were in my parents' car on the riverbank of the same river. My parents had gone fishing, and we were left in the car. I was playing with the gearshift. I shifted the gear and the car rolled backwards down the bank toward the river, stopping at the river's edge.

Thinking back on those kinds of incidents as an adult, how can I not acknowledge God? All the things we did as kids that were life-threatening accidents waiting to happen but they didn't! Why didn't we slip and fall off that pipe into the river and drown? Why didn't the car go into the river? Why am I still here? How can I not be thankful to God for saving me from all the scary life-threatening moments I experienced in my childhood?

ANCESTRAL SPIRITS

ONE explanation is the protection of our ancestral spirits. In our African culture, we credited such moments to our ancestral spirits – relatives who have died but whose unseen spirits are present around us all the time. These relatives know the script of our life, and part of their responsibility as spiritual ancestors is to pluck us out of moments that will interrupt our destiny. They keep reaching in and snatching us out of situations, and we don't know who they are or when they will intercede and keep us safe.

I always felt an overwhelming, all-encompassing and powerful, gentle presence with me. It gave me an air of invincibility and purpose without arrogance. What the purpose of my existence was I had no clue. However, there was always a gentle, driving force moving me. Reflecting back, there had to be only one reason that we survived in spite of the imminent dangers we faced growing up, and that was because there was a purpose to our lives—a destiny to fulfill—and our ancestral spirits were there to protect us. I have kept them very busy in my life!

ASPIRATIONS

WHEN I was a youngster, I wanted to be what every little boy wants to be: a fireman or an astronaut. I never wanted to be a political leader or a preacher. Later, it was a doctor or a teacher. Whether that was the influence of television or something else, I don't know. I may have been influenced by viewing them as symbols of success because they were on TV, but they were all positions of service—doctor, fireman, teacher.

When I looked at these people of service, I saw that they were all white because all the movie stars were white. That was our everyday reality; we didn't see black firemen or black astronauts. We saw white actors in all the roles, but that didn't stop me from visualizing the dream that it could be me. In my mind, I didn't see a white fireman; I saw a fireman.

Our black stars were Amos and Andy, Step and Fetch, or servants for Shirley Temple. Actors all played very stereotypical roles until there was Sidney Poitier in Lilies of the Field, To Sir, with Love, and They Call Me Mr. Tibbs. We had a few other role models: we saw black teachers, because they were in our schools, and there was a black doctor in our neighborhood, and of course, black musicians.

TRADITIONS

SOME of the behaviors that have been passed down in the black culture have come from our African roots. Maybe along the way they have become watered down or twisted around. Perhaps they really weren't modified and we have just accepted those behaviors and they have become traditions.

Through this mentality of tradition without asking why we, out of ignorance, continue an unhealthy behavior. I address asking why when I talk about nutrition. For instance, when I was growing up, we ate every part of the pig. And in Mississippi they still do. Why? People don't stop and question. The usual answer is: "That's what our mother and her mother fixed when we were growing up." Or, maybe the response is, "The tradition has been passed down in my family through generations." In truth, at the time when eating pork started, people were very poor. If they didn't grow it, they didn't eat. Since pigs could be kept in a small area and they would eat any scraps and had many body parts that could be eaten, you raised and ate pork.

This is just one example of why people do things out of cultural habit and have no idea why. Now we have more evidence-based research, information, and knowledge about the ill effects of eating pork. I ask, "Are you willing to teach your kids bad habits even though it means they are going to be sick?" Many of our food and lifestyle habits that are based on traditions have left us with a legacy of health problems. We move less in our day than our great-grandparents did. They had to move, from the time they got up until they went to bed, to function and survive. The bathroom wasn't in the house, and they might have even had to walk to the outhouse! Our lifestyle is completely different. Again I ask, "Are you going to teach your kids an eating habit that's going to make them sick because that's the way your grandparents ate?" Unfortunately, society usually doesn't evolve and change based on the need to be healthy.

Another tradition we accepted was how people address each other. I remember the grocery store owners who were white in a black neighborhood always addressed my parents and grandparents by their first names. My grandparents, who were older than the owners, out of respect would address the owners as Mr. So-and-So and Mrs. So-and-So. I accepted the fact that I had to call them Mr. Frank or Miss Lucy because of their age difference with me. That's what I was taught as being respectful—respect your elders, regardless. I didn't understand why it didn't come back the other way to my grandparents. When I left home in 1973, and went back six or eight years later, the mentality was the same. My grandparents were still calling the owners Mr. or Miss, and the white people were still calling my parents and grandparents by their first names. This seemed disrespectful, but to my grandparents, that was acceptable because that's all they knew.

An example of this conditioning arose on a visit back home in 1992. My dad was proud of me and wanted to introduce me to his white boss at a local hardware store. He was saying to his boss, "Remember I showed you an article in a magazine about Billy Von and now he's on TV." His boss said, "Yes CV he's a big boy." Boy! I was nearly forty years old, and he was still calling me Boy!

My dad was telling him how much I achieved and he responded, "Coloreds in California are really doing big things." Coloreds! All this was said out of respect, but it's the mentality. How could someone not understand the proper term was now black or African-American and had been for 30 years?

Depending on their age, I even accept "colored" from a white person who is older, because, in their day, that term was highly respectful and an endearment. However, someone who is in their 50s and still says "colored?" I can't accept their use of the word. How could they be stuck in that time warp and not know the cultural changes going on around the globe?

MY NEIGHBORHOOD

AS I was growing up, people in my neighborhood were tough and poor. I developed survival methods apart from physical violence and made a conscious choice never to drink or do drugs or join a gang. So, when kids today tell me they have to do these things to be cool, or that they are just a product of their environment, I tell them that they do have the ability to choose. I survived to be an adult role model who said no and didn't lose self-esteem, self-worth, or personal power. And as my childhood friends will attest to, I was still considered cool.

In any neighborhood, there is an established pecking order for power and control. Ours wasn't any different. We had a rough neighborhood. There were bullies more so than gangs. It wasn't big organized gangs like in Chicago, but packs of kids. Sometimes you had a fight on the way to school. Sometimes you had a fight coming home from school. It was that kind of activity in my neighborhood. My folks didn't allow us to run in packs. And I've always been independent, avoiding gangs and most confrontational situations.

When I was 14, I had trouble with one group of guys—more specifically, with the one guy who was the leader of a pack. He had been after me, trying to intimidate me for some time. I always tried to avoid a difficult situation or confrontation. It would always end up that I would either slip by the pack, or they'd miss me after school, or I'd go around the back after a school dance to avoid meeting them. My parents had complained to the police about threats from this group of teens. The police had done nothing. So, my dad told them, "If you won't take care of it, I'll take care of it."

Kemp's Place was a popular, small, one-room café off campus where students could go during lunch period to get something to eat. There was a pay phone on the wall and a counter with stools. It was so small there wasn't any room for tables. At lunch students would go there for burgers. I had two favorite foods I'd order: a chili burger, like they make it in the South, and a cheese honey bun. The honey bun was put on the grill, and cheese was melted over the top.

One day I went there, and the place was packed with students trying to leave to get back to school on time. Suddenly these guys came in, and there's only one way out—the door I came in from. It ended up that they were standing in the doorway and everyone else had left. They blocked the door and wouldn't let me out. I couldn't get back to school. There were threats. I just said, "I need to call my dad at work". I remember this guy saying, "Go ahead and call him because by the time he gets here, it will all be over with anyway."

I used the payphone and called my dad. He instructed me, "Stay there and just go along with whatever they say. I'll be right there." He was walking out the door of the store as he ended the call. Time lapse made it seem like before I could get the phone hung up he was driving up outside. He pulled up, got out of the car, and walked in. He looked at me and said, "Go to school." I walked toward the door where they stood, but hesitated. My dad looked at me and said, "Are you going to listen to them or listen to me? I said go to school." They would not move out of the way.

My dad is a little guy. He was smaller than most of these guys, and they were older than me. However, they had no idea what they were up against. My dad had been a Golden Gloves boxer in the Navy. He grabbed the leader with one hand, shoving him against the wall. I looked at the guy who seemed to be up in the air. I looked down, and his feet weren't even touching the floor. While holding him with one hand, my dad reached in his pocket and pulled out a gun, shoved it literally in his mouth, and pulled back the trigger.

My dad looked at me, "I said to go to school." You should have seen those other guys split. I wasn't about to argue with him either and hustled out. As I passed by his car, I saw he had a rifle on the seat. He'd come with a handgun and a rifle to take care of things. After that, I wasn't bothered for quite a while.

Right across the street from the school was a big park—Magnolia Court. There were houses around the park. You had to walk through the park to get to our side of town. Otherwise, you had to walk a mile out of the way. My mother used to live there after she moved out of her mother's house when she dated my father. While he was courting her, my dad lived several miles away on the other side of town where my grandmother's café was. He would wait until the last minute to leave her, which often meant returning home late after dark. He must have really loved my mother, because it was very dangerous for a black man to get caught on the street after the sun went down.

This was a time of heavy Ku Klux Klan activities and intimidation. My dad would be trying to make it back home in the dark after city curfew, and when he saw a car coming he would have to run and duck behind a pole or a bush so he wouldn't be seen and persecuted, beaten up, taken to jail or killed.

One night Chic, her boyfriend, two of our other friends, and I were together. We were going to walk across the park to get home after the dance. That night a couple of different packs of guys from the neighborhood were waiting for us. They didn't go to our school, so they weren't allowed on the school campus or at our dances. They waited outside the fence that was literally on the street. When we got out of the dance they knew we were going to walk across the park. At first, they were talking trash to be cool, and trying intimidate us.

Things calmed down enough so that we decided to run through the park as fast as we could. It's a dark park, but they were already there. Suddenly it was like Hunger Games. People were scurrying around the park just trying to get through. There were bricks and bottles flying across our heads. We heard people screaming. Then we heard shots being fired. I felt a hit in the knee, but I thought I got hit with a brick. It turned out I had been shot! It just grazed me—bled and hurt like crazy—but it didn't require surgery or medical attention. After we reached home safely we successfully kept the incident from our parents.

CHAPTER 3

The Civil Rights Movement

THROUGHOUT much of America's history there has been a wide gap between the idea of civil rights and the reality of racial injustice. After the Civil War, Jim Crow laws in the South were a network of legislation and customs that dictated the separation of blacks and whites on every level of society. Whites and blacks could not stay at the same hotels, attend the same schools, eat in the same restaurants, be treated in the same hospitals, use the same drinking fountains, use the same telephone booths, use the same parks, or even be incarcerated in the same prisons.

The National Association for the Advancement of Colored People (NAACP) was founded in 1901 in New York City by a group of white and black intellectuals. In 1916 NAACP expanded membership into the South. It attacked segregation and racial inequality through the courts.

Black leaders in the '40s had begun to make inroads with federal laws. On July 26, 1948, President Harry S. Truman signed Executive Order 9981 establishing the President's Committee on Equality of Treatment and Opportunity in the Armed Services, committing the government to integrating the segregated military. This was a big step in the right direction in the civil rights movement.

Civil rights, as a reflection of societal attitudes, are only adopted when large numbers of people demand them. The mid-1950s marked the dawn of a new era of social activism for the attainment of civil rights. Blacks and their supporters were inspired by the words of the Supreme Court in Brown V. the Board of Education in Topeka, Kansas and subsequent decisions in which the court ruled segregation unconstitutional.

Early civil rights efforts of the 1950s and early '60s involved lawsuits, and then the emphasis shifted to civil disobedience and nonviolent demonstrations lead by Dr. Martin Luther King, Jr. and others. From previous experiences, black leaders recognized that laws alone would not change things; people had to take action to ensure that the legal rulings were translated into everyday life. Throughout the 1950s, civil rights organizations, most notably the NAACP, were strengthened, and their members prepared to fight.

In Clarksdale and elsewhere, we lived with fear, though you couldn't touch it or even explain what the fear was. You avoided trouble as much as you could. You didn't go where you were not wanted, because you knew trouble could strike anywhere. You stuck to your neighborhood and obeyed the curfew. Between my neighborhood and downtown there were white neighborhoods. Some of those white neighborhoods started to become integrated with black families as white families started moving out, trying to move farther and farther away. Eventually, those neighborhoods became integrated because white people who didn't have enough money to move, stayed.

However, the white churches were still in those integrated neighborhoods. The whites who would come back to go to church would still not allow black people into their church, even though the church was now in a mostly black neighborhood. I remember being irate about the situation. I went to a Catholic school, and as president of the student council, I felt it was my responsibility to bring this injustice to the attention of the students and teachers. The nuns were some of the main, driving forces behind getting students together to go to the white church. We believed in Dr. Martin Luther King's strategy of nonviolence. Everyone agreed that we should go over and attend church. We "crashed" the church like we would crash a party. We were not welcomed.

Earlier my sister, Chic, and I spent the summers with my mother's older sister in Ohio. My aunt is named Saint as well, and she lived in an integrated neighborhood. That didn't make an impression on me. It was just life. I was adaptable. What was normal for them was normal for me. I never had trouble being a social butterfly. I just joined in and acted like I'd known those people, white or black, my whole life. Yet, when I was back in Mississippi, based on the energy there, without a thought I slipped back into the tradition of segregation.

I had to go up the back stairs when I went to our family physician—up the back, where the fire escape was—and then I had to sit in the black waiting room. The reception area separated the black waiting room from the white waiting room. I could look across the receptionist and see the white people. At the time, I didn't realize anything was wrong with this because my parents seemed to naturally accept the separation. They just sat there like nothing was wrong. It was normal for them. There were black theaters and white theaters and we couldn't go to the white Paramount Theater, although white people came to Roxy, our theater. I was in junior high school before we could go to the white theater.

Once when Chic and I were walking through town with our grandmother, my sister ran ahead and into a bus station where she drank from a "whites only" fountain. Our grandmother was furious and scared. "Why did you do that?" she demanded. My sister said, "I just wanted to see what white water tasted like."

I also remember one day wanting to go into Woolworths and buy a snow cone because it was so hot. But the counter was for whites only.

The civil rights movement didn't happen overnight—it was something I grew up with. In my home, the issue of civil rights was always spoken about. As children, we were aware of things happening because on television we saw lynchings and KKK activities; we learned of the murder of Medgar Evers. In fact, on the property behind a school in Clarksdale, there still existed a hanging block! All of this was real. Segregation was always blatantly in our faces. It was in our life day in and day out, at whatever age we were.

Medgar Evers, a WWII veteran, was field secretary for the NAACP in Mississippi in 1954. He was assassinated in Jackson, Mississippi on June 12, 1963. Following this incident, there was a march on Washington D.C. where King gave what became known as his "I Have a Dream" speech on August 28. Until that time, Dr. King was not well known outside the South. Shortly after his speech came the bombing of churches and homes, and the killing of the four young girls in Birmingham's 16th Street Baptist Church in September. All were significant events in the civil rights movement.

DR. MARTIN LUTHER KING, JR.

THE Southern Christian Leadership Conference (SCLC) was an organization of black ministers formed in 1957. Sixty-five black ministers from 11 states came to Martin Luther King, Sr.'s church in Atlanta, Georgia to form the group. Although only 28 years old at the time, they elected King, Jr. as their first president. King brought to the organization his dedication to social justice and inspired speeches. King's philosophy of nonviolence was a combination of ideas from the teachings of Jesus, the writings of Henry David Thoreau on civil disobedience (or disobeying laws believed to be cruel or unjust), and Mahatma Gandhi's beliefs and methods of using nonviolent strategies. King's tactics included boycotts, sit-ins, and strikes. The idea of nonviolent protests was accepted by other black leaders. They agreed the use of such methods would bring needed change in achieving freedom for all people.

Dr. King and other black leaders began a national campaign of nonviolent, civil disobedience, using marches and demonstrations to bring the injustice of discrimination and segregation to the attention of the public. A secondary goal with nonviolence was to show the world the dignity, discipline, and dedication with which the blacks conducted their boycotts, and the unity of the black communities to end the injustice of segregation and obtain voter rights.

Clarksdale was active in the civil rights movement, and on May 29, 1958, Martin Luther King, Jr. visited Clarksdale for the first major meeting of the Southern Christian Leadership Conference. The number one associate of Dr. King in Clarksdale was Aaron E. Henry. In 1960, Henry, a local pharmacist, was named state president of the NAACP and went on to organize a two-year long boycott of Clarksdale businesses. Frequently a target of racist violence, Henry was arrested in Clarksdale repeatedly and, in one famous incident, was chained to the rear of a city garbage truck and led through the streets of Clarksdale to jail. We are not talking about the 1930s here. This was how bad things were in the '60s and '70s.

Henry was a family friend. His pharmacy was literally a couple of doors down from my grandmother's café in the heart of our world. His children went to school with us. Henry and Dr. King were a presence in our lives as they spoke at our churches, calling us to action.

In 1962, Dr. King visited Clarksdale on the first stop of a region-wide tour, where he urged the crowd to "stand in, sit in, and walk by the thousands." These marches and demonstrations brought attention to the cause of civil rights and led to moral outrage nationwide, bringing the beginning of a change in public attitude.

I knew Dr. King. He didn't come up to me and scoop me up and put me on his shoulders, but I remember hearing him speak. I don't recall a lot about what he said, other than being aware of his dynamic energy and direct involvement in the movement itself. I sensed King's passion, but it wasn't unique, because Mr. Henry had the same passion. All of our Baptist ministers had the same fire, so when Dr. King came in, he didn't stand out. What he said was nothing new to us. Pastors announced from the pulpit every Sunday that they would observe boycotts and support protests and urged everyone in the congregation to do the same. What we saw in all black leaders, not only Dr. King, were people passionate about their mission. This came through in the way they spoke, in their energy, and in their commitment to civil rights for all, not just blacks.

Another leader from our neighborhood was Charles Espy who was the first black person appointed to the school board in Clarksdale. He went on to become the first African-American to serve as a city commissioner and first black mayor of Clarksdale, serving for many, many years. He was also president of the U.S. Conference of Black Mayors. I knew of his political connections and impact. I knew him, because he was in our neighborhood. Members of my family were close friends of his and his family, but I didn't know him personally as he was of my parents' generation.

Aaron Henry and Charles Espy as colleagues of Dr. King, and in conjunction with the NAACP, organized a march to Clarksdale Public High School in the name of desegregation. The city public high school had no ethnic minorities in the school. It was run by the city, paid for with our taxes, but only white students were allowed to attend, and it had been that way for years. This was to be a major march in the city, and we were given a date when we were to meet at various churches, and then we would all march to the school and tell them: "We want to go to school."

MY PART

I was part of the demonstration to desegregate our city schools that day in 1968 when I was 14. Certain people were chosen to be in the front of the crowd. I was one of those because, as 8th grade class president, I was representing the school.

We marched through downtown and stood out in front of the school. Of course, the police were there. But we stood on the street and the school administrator came out to the steps. Quite clearly, I remember him saying: "You have to leave now because you are on public private property." I think to this day his words were why I became an English major in college. Public private, how can it be private if it's public? I asked myself.

The administrator told us we had to leave or be arrested, so we left. That night we met again at various churches and sang songs like, This Little Light of Mine, We Shall Overcome, We Shall Not Be Moved, and Lift Every Voice. The civil rights leaders told us we would march again the next day, and we had to be prepared to go to jail. Going to jail was our commitment for making a statement in the name of desegregation.

The next day we marched to the school and stood in the street. I was again in the front line. The police were there. The National Guard was there. The leaders said "now ", and we all stepped onto the campus and were all arrested. We didn't go inside the building or anything, just stepped on the grounds. At 14, or even if you were four years old, your age didn't matter—if you stepped on the white campus, you went to jail.

The police handcuffed us and put as many of us as possible in paddy wagons. There were too many people. The solution was to put a barricade around the crowd and make them march to the jail. There were at least 1,000 people, too many for the jailhouse, so the rest were put in the jail yard with guard dogs. I was arrested; I went to jail. The NAACP was working very fast to get us released. I was booked in the county jail—my only time in jail—and was there barely overnight. Finally, in 1969, schools were federally ordered to desegregate. I was 15.

As whites became involved in the civil rights movement, it was different for them than for us. Whether their participation was out of human compassion or whether it was the guilt of their forefathers, there was a different energy. I'm not saying their passion and commitment wasn't real.

However, when you have someone say, "I started walking this journey even before I was born," they were born into the journey. That was the case with me. I was not given the option of whether I was going to be involved or not. I was born into it. It was my life from the onset. The struggle was mine as a birthright. We had lived with a constant energy of injustice and violence for years.

To have someone who is not black get involved and commit was different. They weren't "born into" the journey. It was a very conscious decision on their part to support civil rights. Nevertheless, their willingness to go to jail, to be attacked, to be as "all the way in" as they possibly could be was commendable. On June 2, 1964, the KKK's killing of three civil rights workers registering voters near Philadelphia, Mississippi helped encourage the civil rights movement, and whites became more aware of, and interested, in the situation.

INJUSTICE

THERE are basically two things I remember that had an impact on me regarding the civil rights movement. First, there was a cause, with its movement to cure injustice and make change. Second, there was the question, what would you do to survive? That is, survive the time that was the nucleus of the cause.

I remember the music of the era—how Stack records and Motown were getting big, and that sound kept the energy flowing in our neighborhoods, in our families and for the cause. Growing up right in the heart of that has chiseled some of my character. This mentality of race against race in Mississippi is something that encouraged me to leave.

As I looked at the people who owned all the buildings in Clarksdale, I realized every building was owned by white people. There were black people living and running small businesses in them, but the buildings were all falling down, roach-infected, and owned by whites. Blacks paid high rents to live and work under these conditions. I had a problem with the mentality of what we were conditioned to accept, not only as the norm, but how this prevailing attitude was acceptable. As I looked around at the city and state, I felt that the whole world couldn't possibly be like this. I couldn't accept that this was the way life was everywhere.

During the civil rights movement, it was the injustice of segregation that we heard about the most. That's what was on the news, what we heard in our churches from the pulpit, and found on the posters on telephone poles. Injustice was the issue.

What I saw was the communication dynamics already spoken about between my grandparents and the white people of the city. I saw their social standing or placement, and to me something was wrong with how my grandparents were treated. The pecking order of how they were addressed, based on their age, even, was wrong; when a 13-year old white teen would speak to my 70-year old grandmother like she was 12 and call her "Girl." It was this type of attitude that had a feeling of injustice. One of my favorite quotes of the journey is: "Injustice anywhere is injustice everywhere."

From the civil rights experience I did receive an education. From meetings in the churches, I learned organizational strategies and the boundaries of nonviolence set by Dr. King: what we were going to do, how we were going to do it, the timetable of what was going to happen and the probable outcomes. Being peripherally involved in the whole strategy as it developed and watching not one person step away from the commitment taught me that the goal is always bigger than the struggle. We were told there are going to be problems, there are going to be dogs, there are going to be arrests, there are going to be policemen with batons, tear gas and fire hoses and mass arrests. All these elements are going to be present. They explained this would be the immediate consequence of the action we took, the results of our immediate commitment and struggle. When we walked to the campus with Dr. King, we could take pride that the goal was bigger than someone being arrested, bigger than being attacked by dogs, bigger than being shot.

From my involvement in the civil rights movement, I took away an understanding of the importance of committing to an ideal that is bigger than yourself, something that affects mankind. When you know it's the right thing to do, according to your inner self, be involved instead of standing back and watching injustice happen. Get involved on purpose. I learned there is strength in unity. I learned that one person can make a difference. These are things I implement in my life right now, to this day, decades later. I learned from King's teachings that love is the only way. You can't put out a small fire with a bigger fire. You can't put out a big fire with an inferno. I also took to heart what Martin Luther King, Jr. said: "Take a stand and lift a voice."

I knew the cause wasn't about anyone personally, it was about injustice. I see this missing in the youth today. They don't understand the word "cause." A cause impacts humanity overall, not just someone as an individual.

The example of the goal being bigger than the struggle filters all through my life. The completion of high school and graduating was bigger than all the little struggles I had trying to make it to graduation. It is the same when you are preparing for a concert with all the practices and rehearsals; your fingers are hurting, they are bleeding, you are missing meals, and you can't go out and be with your friends. But all of this work leads up to the performance. For many of us, that work is a process of development that requires discipline and sacrifice. Yet the goal we are striving toward is bigger than the journey itself.

I know these ideals of commitment and getting involved in a cause are not being taught to children today. There were attitudes and responsibilities that held the cultures together 50 years ago that are not present in some of the youth today. There were elements of cohesiveness back then that are absent now. Growing up we had boundaries. This seems to be the same with all cultures—black kids, white kids, Latin and Asian kids. Cultural values of personal responsibility have given way to attitudes of entitlement. And if entitlement doesn't happen, then self-pity comes into play. Today it's a mentality of self-interest versus that of a village consciousness. Teens don't have a cause bigger than they are. This is a global phenomena, not just here in the USA or among blacks. It's a sign of the times around the world.

Parents and parenting were different 50 years ago too. If materialism is not the precise cause of this shift in orientation we are experiencing, it is a major contributing factor to this attitude of freedom free of personal responsibility. I travel all over the world, and I see this attitude in every culture. Some of the cultures that are more Eastern than Western are fighting to hold on to the concept of personal responsibility, but in Western culture, it is mostly gone.

THE SNAKE

LACK of personal responsibility is a vicious circle. It reminds me of the symbol of the snake eating its own tail. Freedom with a lack of ethical and moral responsibility accompanied with an entitlement attitude has created a circle that is destroying itself.

I say that, yet, I fought for freedom. I went into the military during a war. I know what fighting for freedom is about. I know what it takes to live in a country and society that says you have the right to be your own person, to live well, to take advantage of opportunities, to use the tools you have to produce success in your own life. But when that freedom infringes on the rights of others, it's like the snake eating its own tail.

When I see a young person acting way out of line – maybe he is threatening another child or doing something self-destructive or illegal – I can expect that his parents will come get in my face if I try to discipline him. "Who do you think you are… Don't you ever talk to my kid… If you've got something to say to my kid, you say it to me." And what does that do? It gives the adolescent a lot of power, power they don't know how to manage.

When I say "freedom," I mean those freedoms that hold us together as a democratic society and constitute our right to be who we are. Freedom requires discipline. Discipline and respect must be taught. These values have to come from somewhere because without them we eat our own tail.

Raising children is difficult, especially during the years of adolescence when young people are testing the waters. Here in America, children of that age have so much freedom. This is not necessarily a positive thing.

There is all this newness in adolescence: new hormones, new emotions, new situations in their environment. How much experience do adolescents have managing huge concepts, including boundaries and the values I consider important? The answer is none.

I ask, "Why are children absent of these values?" I have to look to the parents or family, or community or village, or the system—the government or state. Who else is there? The parents say, "Well, I didn't get those values when I was growing up either." Then I look at their parents, because you can't teach your kids what you don't have. So, the younger parents are doing the best they can with the tools they have, which are lacking.

At some point in the history of our society, material goods became valued more than people. And the single-parent income didn't meet the cost of living. This caused a paradigm shift, where for the average family, two incomes are needed to survive. I mean to survive, not live well. So, both parents go to work to make sure they protect materialistic commodities and our most precious commodity—that is, our kids— became secondary. My worst fear is losing the children of this world.

In the era of the civil rights movement, the things that were taught to us gave a different perspective on value, of what's valuable. Freedom is valuable. Human rights are valuable. Unity is valuable. Love is valuable.

I'm not sure if you walk up to the average student today and mention any of those concepts he or she will say they are valuable. They are not as valuable as the latest shoes, the latest gadgets, or the latest video game.

The schools are now put in the position of being the parent. That will never work. Schools were never intended to work that way. Schools are an academic, education-based institution. They can only specialize in doing well what they are designed and built to do—educate, not parent.

As an example, a bank is an economic institution specializing in economy, numbers, and currency. That's its role and field of expertise. If you take the medical field, and start making banks responsible for medical treatment, what is going to happen to sick people? Likewise, when you expect teachers to be parents, and parents give all the power to their youngsters who are not mature enough to handle the freedoms they are given, you have a mess on your hands.

I understand that when parents get home from working all day they are too tired to invest in our most precious commodity. They have given their hearts, time, souls, energy and emotions to the materialistic commodities at the cost of our children going un-nurtured. For a variety of reasons, more mothers today are electing to stay home with their small children. I see this as a healthy trend.

ASSASSINATIONS

MY Catholic school was small—one class per grade. I was nine when President John F. Kennedy was assassinated on November 22, 1963. I remember being at school; it was a cool and cloudy day. I recall the assassination was very upsetting to the nuns. It became one of those days when the world stopped rotating. I remember the shock. It produced such a dramatic shift in energy. The energy shift went through the school like a wave. The older students understood more about what the assassination meant. We younger ones knew who the President was, and I understood the impact. I just didn't really understand the intimate details. Initially there was silence, and the radio was on to follow the news. It was such a shocking event all the classes were dismissed early.

Dr. King was assassinated during the hardcore era of the civil rights movement on April 4, 1968. It happened 70 miles away in Memphis. Blacks in the South lived with violence for years. There was so much uproar and shooting during the civil rights movement that we were witnessing violence all the time. Violence was such a constant energy in my environment, for it to go one step further wasn't unrealistic.

King's assassination was shocking, but with King it was different than with JFK. President Kennedy's event had a different energy to it, not just in the school but in the community. With the murder of King, I felt a real dynamic energy coming from the white population in the South that was almost celebratory. Even though it would not have been tolerated if spoken like that, there was an undercurrent I could feel.

It was another very dark, dark day for us, because we had a direct relationship to Dr. King. This made his death personal as opposed to the President, who we'd never met. King had been in and out of Clarksdale. I'm not sure what happened in the public schools but in our school, responses turned immediately to tributes to King and his work. School was let out as a sign of reverence.

It is hard to believe that was nearly 50 years ago. Students today live a life removed from this history. When my daughter, Kenna, was nine, she was in a play with me. It was about Martin Luther King, Jr. and civil rights. The cast was all adults except for her. Kenna's part was to represent the spirit of the four young girls who were killed in the Birmingham church in 1967. I wanted Kenna to understand why her part in this production was important. I rented Spike Lee's 4 Little Girls, a moving documentary about the 16th Street Baptist Church bombing that killed the four girls. We watched it, and Kenna would make some comment, like "Where are the black policemen?" When the documentary was over, she said, "Can I watch cartoons now?" I stopped her and said, "No, we need to talk about this." I explained how important the death of those little girls was in getting white parents involved in the civil rights movement. I was serious, but gentle with Kenna as I really wanted her to understand why she was in the play and why her part was important.

DISCRIMINATION

DISCRIMINATION was what it was, and it is still with us today. I am no stranger to discrimination. Unfortunately, as the years passed, I found the rest of the world was often as prejudiced as the South—it was just, and is, more subtle elsewhere.

At one point, I was traveling from Sacramento to Stockton to audition for a part in a dinner theatre production. That night I stopped at a convenience store in Lodi, a small town between the two cities. Inside the shop were white guys making aggressive racially prejudiced remarks. Others guys walked in and started calling me the "N" word. And I was thinking, "Do I know you?" No one else in the store seemed to be shocked by this behavior—it appeared to be an everyday conversation. I felt extremely unsafe and decided not to fuel the flame and kept my emotions under control. I quickly paid for what I had selected and left.

This was my first smack of reality in liberal California. I knew prejudice exists everywhere, yet it had not been my experience in Los Angeles, San Francisco, and Sacramento itself.

Here in California, prejudice is subtle. Today biracial couples are, by and large, accepted in liberal California. Still, not everyone accepts such a couple. Back in the late '70s, interracial couples weren't the norm outside of my circle of friends in the entertainment world. In Sacramento, my first girlfriend was white and her father was racially biased. She could have been acting out against her father by dating me. I don't know, but I don't believe she was prejudiced. I think her mother kept the concept of prejudice away from her as much as possible as she was growing up. The first time we witnessed racial prejudice together she appeared to be extremely shocked. I was dropping her off one evening at her parents' rural home, and we saw a burning cross on their property. After that, she began to recall things that had been said in jest as she was growing up. She started putting these comments together and discovered that these weren't jokes. She began remembering little moments of conversations with her father indicating prejudice, but at the time, she was naïve to the intention behind them.

I have been the subject of racial profiling. When our dance and fitness studio, Step 1, opened a satellite location in the Sacramento suburb of Carmichael, I taught classes there two nights a week and was usually late to arrive. Staff would say, "Come on, just leave earlier". Unbeknown to them, I was being profiled and frequently stopped by the police. I never shared with the staff why I was often late.

However, my experiences of discrimination have been limited. Greg King, a colleague, recounts, "We did some school assemblies at different locations over the course of a year's time. Pepper and I and the rest of the team take pride in reaching over 10,000 students in less than a year. Never once have I seen any type of prejudice from him or others to him. I can't recall, as much as I've been around Pepper, someone approaching him in that manner."

There were also a couple of instances with the dance company where subtle prejudice occurred. Owners with businesses would have a problem with other black dancers being in the company. I'm not a complainer or one to make waves, so I never said anything.

I have also experienced the reverse. On occasion, I have been criticized by others in the dance world for appealing to mainstream audiences. I always look to do things that appeal to many, many people, not a certain ethnic group. My message is one of unity, wellness and positivity.

I feel the greatest struggle in life facing the black community is not so much discrimination, but taking responsibility for our own dreams, choices, family, and communities. Maintaining self-respect, having respect for others, focusing more on keeping God first in our lives, and teaching our children through example by being good role models is the most important undertaking. We must teach all students early in life the importance of education, inspiration, self-motivation and courage. We must provide them with resources, support their efforts, and praise their accomplishments.

CHAPTER 4
Coming of Age

ALTHOUGH I was the student body president in high school, I wasn't a leader all the time. I've been graced with a certain energy in that people have been willing to listen to me and want to be around me. It's always been my mentality and my character to thrive in whatever situation I am in which has led to leadership positions. Others are drawn to the type of energy I have. My intention was never to use this attraction for power or prestige.

My internal motivation was always present, propelling me to reach for the top. As a young martial artist, I didn't feel complete until I was a black belt. When I was singing in the church choir, I had to become the choir director.

Where there were opportunities that caught my attention, or looked like fun, that's where the magic happened for me. In subjects that excited me, whether it was music or martial arts, I didn't have to be pushed to put in the time and discipline to excel.

There is a certain internal element that has to drive the work in order for us to reach our highest potential in everything we do. For the most part, we don't read about something in a book and decide, "Okay, I'm off and running." Internal motivation is required. Some people are born with it. I don't ever remember not being this way. I always wanted the feeling of others being proud of me. I don't remember all the specific events but I remember the feeling of my father, mother, grandmother and others saying, "Oh, that's so awesome. I love you." It was a good feeling so I would seek more approval. That feeling gave me the extra push to excel.

I am very success oriented and would also seek success even if it was just for me. In grade school I was a horrible speller. I spelled words the way they sounded or were introduced to me. This was not how the words were correctly spelled. It produced such frustration for me being around old folks who spoke with a strong dialect and then trying to read when the words on the page weren't the way I had heard them.

One of my goals at a young age was to learn to speak more clearly, grammatically correct, more fluently. I made this conscious decision even before high school.

I didn't work on purpose to get rid of my Mississippi accent, but in the process of learning to spell correctly and read, that's what happened. My interests have always leaned toward English. Math and science were also strong subjects for me. Geography and history—no, I'm not good at dates and events. Maybe this is because I rarely look at my life in a rearview mirror. Besides, I can see a lot more clearly with my glasses on my face rather than behind my head. I have always looked forward.

DARK DAYS

FOR the most part, I think we have events in our life so that others can learn from our survival of those experiences. There were challenging situations that made me who I am. That goes for everyone. Whether or not you are willing to learn from these experiences or share them doesn't change their purpose. To decide to share the purpose of them is a completely different thing. There are things that I know other people experience that are not unique to me. For example, I didn't grow up with my mother and father in the same household. I remember the day my father left. As a youngster, that was a really dark day.

I remember the day in high school when I was told my girlfriend—who I never touched because we were waiting for marriage—was raped and got pregnant. That was another really dark day. At the time, you don't know how to manage the emotions you've never experienced before. When you try to, and you don't have the tools, you go into survival mode. That's the natural inclination of any living thing. It doesn't matter whether it's an animal or human being. That's the first innate response, unless you've been trained otherwise.

My girlfriend didn't tell me until after she found out she was pregnant. Initially, I wanted to kill the guy. I knew where a gun was, got it and left to go find him. That was my first reaction. She would have gone completely without ever saying anything, but discovering she was pregnant she had to confess. It ended up she had not been raped, but that was the story she gave me at the time.

Eventually it came out she got tired of waiting for me, because I wouldn't touch her. One day she skipped school and went to this guy's house. He was a year older and went to public school. One thing led to another. She couldn't come to me with that story. She had to put herself in the victim role. She didn't think she'd cause that strong of a reaction in me. She knew my reaction would be bad, but not so bad that I was going to kill him.

Fortunately, I had to walk several miles from my neighborhood to where the guy's house was. I had to pass my grandmother's café. I had to pass by my dad's work. People who've been around me a long time recognize when I "lock in." I get a certain look, and nothing can stop me.

My girlfriend was hysterical but had enough presence of mind to call my dad at the supermarket. Before I could get to the store, he was already on the street waiting for me in his long, white butcher's apron. He started talking to me. I heard words: "wah, wah, wah." Nothing was penetrating. It got to the point that my dad recognized a calm, conversational approach was not working, so he literally had to get physically aggressive to get the gun from me. "Now I'm not asking you; I'm telling you to give me the gun." That's what I needed, because the other option would not have ended well. I would have killed someone and gone to prison over something that wasn't true.

My dad realized I had all this pent-up rage inside me. Even when I gave him the gun, he knew the rage was still there. He took off his apron and took me down to the juke joint. It was during the day, so I went in and played drums for hours until my rage was spent. My dad literally saved my life that day. And so did music. I beat the drums instead of myself or the other guy to get the rage out.

That incident taught me a lot. It made me recognize we all have that potential to kill someone. I was a good person, and yet I found that potential in myself. Whatever the right moment is and the right emotions, if all the stars are in alignment, and everything converges at the same time, we are all capable of killing.

I had access to a gun, because we had guns in the household. This was normal as there was a lot of intimidation going on around us. We had to be prepared to defend ourselves from the KKK, bogeymen, and people coming to our door with black faces on, sneaking around the house and peeking in the windows. In this situation, my father was going to do what he had to do to save me. When I was ready to hear him, then we talked and talked it out. My dad sustained me through that experience—my schooling and my church upbringing were immaterial at that point.

OTHER INCIDENTS

IN another incident when I was ten, I was raped by one of my mother's friends. My dad was gone from the house. I remember the blood on the sheets, thinking it was all my fault. The woman was an adult, she was my mom's friend, and I was going to be in so much trouble.

After I was raped, there were no answers to any of my questions to ease my emotional pain. I didn't tell my mom, and my dad wasn't living with us. My mom went to her grave never knowing about what her friend did. To this day my dad doesn't know.

I almost told my dad a couple of years later when I was 12. It was time for me to be baptized. I didn't want to become baptized, because I was mad at God. I remember asking my dad, "What if I said I wanted to be baptized because everybody in church was acting happy for me to take this step and I said, 'I believe,' but I really don't want to be baptized?"

And my dad said, "You can't lie. You can't go in the water and lie." But we never dove into why I said those things or had those feelings. I was baptized and lived. Later in my life, it was moments like these that set me up to be able to work with teens that have had the same or similar experiences.

Once I got my mom's gun, and I found myself sitting in the middle of the living room floor thinking, "Life hurts too much." I was just a kid, and no one was home but me. I don't remember any specific thing that clicked in my head to take me out of that situation. I don't remember saying, "This is crazy; I'm not going to do it," or hearing a knock on the door, or anything in my mind. Somehow the moment passed. I don't know what made me get up and put the gun back instead of shooting myself. I just know I put the gun back. There are moments when I think – Why? All I can say is thank goodness for my ancestral spirits.

I knew in my neighborhood, just like any other poor neighborhood in the world, survival was the key. I knew that if I didn't take responsibility for getting myself out, I would probably never leave home and would die sooner if I'd stayed. I signed up for the Air Force before I graduated. I went directly from high school to basic training in the Air Force.

THE AIR FORCE

EVEN though it was during the draft, I didn't wait to be drafted. I volunteered for the military. Did I volunteer because I was excited to go overseas and defend the country by killing people? No, not at all. It was a business deal to me—it was my ticket out of Clarksdale. I knew what I put on the line was my life: years of my life to serve and follow orders and be their puppet for a certain amount of time. I committed to that. Did I want something from them? Absolutely.

I knew there was a system in place already where you got a job, got training, you were fed, clothed and housed every day, and when you got out you could get an education and a home. The trade-off was enlisting and serving out my time by showing up every day and doing what they said. You didn't even have to be the best at what you did! But for me, if I'm going to do something it's all the way in or all the way out; so, I knew when I went in, I was all the way in.

Coming into the military as a black youth from the South, I wasn't given much respect. Kids like me tend to take their emotional triggers with them into the service where they are broken down immediately. You learn those triggers don't carry any weight in your new team. Military service was the first opportunity black men had as an equal opportunity. Under those circumstances, you train and you serve. If you get caught up in an ethnic-based trigger, everybody dies. That's how fragile the situation can be. You can't afford to bring those emotional triggers into that life. You begin to learn your color or education doesn't matter to others, because they may need you to save their life. Or you may need them to save your life. Everybody quickly understands this.

Military life was okay as far as I was concerned. Discrimination was not a burden there. That's when I became aware in my head I could choose to live in an integrated world. That doesn't mean there wasn't segregation present, but I could choose to live above it.

Before going in, I signed up to become a medic. If the training you ask for is available and if your test scores support that, then the Air Force tries to put you where you want to be, because you'll be more committed. I wanted medical training and my math and science scores supported that. When I finished basic training, I went to medical school to become a medic in a medevac helicopter. I trained as an Emergency Medical Technician. Back in the day of my training, EMTs did a lot of what paramedics are doing now—today, paramedics tend to work more as firefighters. At every station I went to over the next six years, I was an EMT. I went from Lackland to Japan to serve in medical evacuations.

For me, being of service and aiding the wounded with compassion was my goal. This service was outside of national wars and beyond politics—it all boiled down to human-to-human. And to me that's what service is about. The oath of the MASH units says, "It doesn't matter who the patient is. If they are the enemy, you treat them because first, they are human beings." Connecting with that ideal worked for me. I didn't think of the war as a war or killing, but rather as the opportunity to be of service to human beings who were suffering.

Being a medic was something I had a passion for before I went in. I loved the job every minute of every day. Whether it was as a field medic or in the hospital emergency room, it didn't matter; it was very fulfilling for me. Duties rotated around shifts similar to a fireman's shift. You don't fight a towering inferno fire every day. Some days you do; other days it's a garage fire. Some days you are doing things around the fire station when you aren't called out.

THE ANTIWAR MOVEMENT

THE antiwar movement didn't affect me. I understood why protestors did what they did. I saw both sides of the issue and understood; there are things that happen in the land of war we don't want to know happen. In our justice system, there are things that are very unjust, things our country would never stand for, things our flag doesn't stand for, but you are commanded to do them in war. It doesn't make you proud, but you do them. For all the right reasons, you may do something that is against your personal beliefs. I am not saying that makes these things right, but you do them.

There is situational ethics and honor. In the middle of a war in a country where, on the average, you would have pointed a gun at 10 or 12-year-olds, marched them to safety and interrogated them later, in another situation you may blow them away right then and there before they have a chance to kill you. In some cases, 10-year-olds were carrying machine guns and setting off mines. You can come to terms with this or you can get caught up with issues such as: what is your personal honor, what is your duty to your country, what are your morals or ethics as a human being? Everyone has the right to determine what those answers are for themselves.

I chose to go into the Air Force and agreed to abide by their rules when I was in the service. Out of the service, I choose differently. There is a lot of pride in being an American when you are part of the team, you feel your presence is for all the right reasons, and you are making a difference in freedom on planet Earth. How much of that is brainwashing? We don't know, but you feel pride in your core, and every time you see red, white and blue, it hits you deeply, and you feel very patriotic. You fight to open the doors for people to have what we have in the arena of freedom and justice. Yet, not everyone in the world understands these concepts.

When you get back home, you see a lot is taken for granted. Patriotism is in songs and words but not in practice. There are a certain number of people who are very supportive of your service. People acknowledge and thank you for your sacrifice, but that isn't everybody. You come back to find ethnic prejudices of all kinds and discover that money runs everything. It is easy for people to sit back and watch things on television and form their opinions when war isn't their reality.

When all the dust clears, it is really about your own self. How do you feel about that time on your journey? How do you feel about what you had control over and what you didn't have control over? Most people don't think this deeply.

RETURNING VETS

IN our society, unfortunately, money rules, and it is not a priority to funnel money into programs to help returning vets. I am frustrated about this. We are talking about life-long problems as a result of their service to our nation.

There are things that keep our system far from being perfect. Strangely, if I'm walking across the street and get hit by a bus, there are more rehabilitation programs to take care of me than if I fight for our country and end up with some traumatic injury.

Everyone deserves to be well and cared for, yet often in this country, because of greed, we tend not make this a priority.

THE GI BILL

THE GI bill was initially the reason I went into the Air Force. I knew at a young age that I wanted to go to college. I knew my parents couldn't afford to send me. I knew the service was my way to get a college education and get out of Clarksdale. I knew it would be a trade-off, but I was willing to do it.

In my town, you could figure out how to leave and be successful, but if you stayed, you didn't have as many options. Every time I went back to Clarksdale, fewer and fewer of us from my graduating class were alive. Many were in prison, or I'd find them on the streets. Too many didn't make it.

Once you were stationed somewhere, you have your shift, like a regular job, and then you would have time off and your own life. I was assigned to emergency room staff, and I wanted to take advantage of my GI bill to take college classes in my free time. I began to take classes wherever I was stationed—usually my tour of duty was for two years. This enabled me to move forward in obtaining more degrees.

MY DECISION-MAKING PROCESS

MY life and my thought process, my consciousness, have always worked for me, even though it may be unorthodox for someone else outside looking in. Most of the decisions I've made and experiences on my path make sense to me. They all seem to fall under the greater umbrella of service.

At the end of the day, for me, decision-making is about listening to your internal radar – that internal something that either forces you to pay attention or ignore it. Some call it your gut, or listening to an inner voice, or your intuition. It's conscious decision-making involving your heart and soul. You know when a decision just feels right. Any time I have tried to put a square peg in a round hole, it has been because I ignored that feeling, and it didn't quite work out.

I am a Taurus, so I can be rather persistent or, as some would say, stubborn. I can take a square peg and pound it into a round hole using a hammer, chiseling it on the sides, sanding it down, and it will go in – but it is not going to be pretty. There are no nice, rounded edges, the hole is destroyed, and the peg is all scarred up. You stand back and say to yourself, "It sure took a lot of effort to come out like that!" So, you learn to hear the voice. You pay attention to the voice of inner fire. It is a blessing to be able to listen to that voice. We all have access to it, but most people have not learned to acknowledge it, or listen to it, or trust it.

Life is a huge chess game and we are the pieces, not the players! On the spiritual level, or whatever you choose to call that plane, there are predetermined strategies about what plays need to occur for you to win the game of life. The pieces on the board are not the strategist; they are the moving parts. Everything you are going to need was already in your packet when you were born. Every skill, tool, ability, insight, talent, and gift is on loan to you so that you can make the moves necessary to capture the king. Other plays and pieces will come along and bump you or make you move in a certain direction in your journey.

In my life, I consider my talents on loan and pray I share them to uplift others. Everything is on loan to us so we can accomplish our mission. We need to acknowledge that and to say, "Let me not get selfish about my gifting." Though on loan, I use the word "mine," because they are mine to use. I can go to Hertz and rent a car and say I'm going to drive my car to the left. The car is on loan to me. It doesn't belong to me but is on loan to me to get from point A to point B in order to accomplish something. But I don't own the car. When I use my talents selfishly, then I have forgotten they are just on loan to me from a higher source to be used in the service of others.

TOPS IN BLUE

WHEN I was stationed in Tokyo I did off-duty things like my MMA matches and playing "Soul Train" in nightclubs around downtown Tokyo. These were separate from my military duty—in my off hours. I was performing most of the time I was in Japan.

My last two years in the military were spent in entertainment. Tops in Blue is the touring entertainment group of the Air Force that originally formed as a special unit in 1953. Generally, the troupe consists of 24 airmen (two or three of whom are women) who perform at bases around the world. The selection process requires winning five rounds of auditions and usually involves about 8,000 contestants, all of whom are active Air Force personnel.

Being raised around music, entertainment and entertainers, and receiving dance training when I was young, I have always been connected to music. I always had a guitar in my barracks. When the opportunity came around between college courses and medic duties to audition for Tops in Blue, I thought, "Why not? It would be fun to be part of a world showcase."

I auditioned, and I knew the odds were against being selected. First of all, you couldn't just sing if you were a singer. Or you couldn't just be a dancer. If you went in as a dancer, you had to sing, dance and play one instrument. Singers also had to be able to dance and play an instrument. If you went in as a musician, you had to play three instruments and sing and dance. And they were only going to choose 24 out of the worldwide Air Force. To put this in perspective, in 2012 there were 332,854 active airmen.

At the audition, you had to come in with something unique, something the judges didn't see every day. I thought trying out would be fun. But my nature is to not lose. I don't do halfway—that would never do. 1978 was the era of Star Wars, so I came up with a costume idea using Christmas lights. The costume actually plugged into the wall with a 100-foot extension cord. If I were doing the same thing today, the lights would be easily operated by batteries and be LED lights. Back in the day, these were real Christmas tree lights. It was one of those costumes that from the audience, or a distance from the stage, looked amazing. You didn't want to see it up close though—it didn't look so good.

When I won the first round of auditions, I thought, "Oh, that's pretty doable." I just kept going, and I reached the next level. And within my unit, everybody was encouraging me. That's like someone from your hometown on American Idol reaching the finals. Everyone in town cheers for the contestants and is proud of them even if they don't know them personally. I started to feel that from my unit—the same thing I felt when I was little, from my family. I kept winning and eventually made the troupe.

Winning was one thing. Then the real work began. Each team starts with a 45-day intensive training period designed to turn the winners into world-class entertainers and prepare them mentally and physically for the tour schedule. At Lackland AFB in Texas we rehearsed 15-18 hours a day, rotating between music and dance coaches. Every day troupe members re-dedicated themselves to being better and working as a team. In 1978 we toured from April 21 to August 27, presenting 143 performances in 130 days. The costume I auditioned in became part of the show.

Besides performing, everyone had stage duties—setting up and taking down the stage sets, looking after the costumes and props, being a technician who sets up the special and visual effects. I was the stage manager, choreographer, and played in the band, even though I was a dancer and singer.

As stage manager, every time we went into a location, I was first off the bus. I decided where the band was going to be set up on stage, where the microphones and music stands were placed. In addition to acting as stage manager, I was sometimes the lead dancer, choreographer for some of the vocal groups and dancers, sang in some of the vocals as the Temptations or the Four Tops, and during certain sets, I would sit in as the drummer in the band. I was fully engaged.

You can't have a string of performances without humorous incidents. Once when I was on the world tour with Tops in Blue, on stage in front of a packed audience, I sang with my fly open the whole number! You feel the draft. You don't want to look; you think "Oh, no." You know everyone in the front row has noticed. My fly being down upstaged everything. In the choreography, there was a step where we would cross our legs, spin, and come back around and grab the microphone. As I spun around, I zipped up. The audience started laughing.

They were enamored that I was so slick and worked zipping up into the choreography—it was perfect timing. I didn't miss a beat.

There was also another incident. We didn't have wireless microphone systems back then. We'd have six microphones all lined up on the stage, with each cord coming down, plugged into the next one and finally going to an electrical source. During one dance my foot got caught in one of the microphone wires. They were all live. There was nothing I could do but watch them cascade like dominoes. The stage manager ran out and tried to catch them as they screeched but just couldn't stop them from falling.

Despite the fact that everyone auditions as a solo act, the biggest lesson I learned in Tops in Blue was teamwork. As an individual, you come in as your own person and transition into becoming part of a unit, part of a world-touring team with one common goal. You quickly come to understand that if, for any reason, your part of the show is missing, then the team is lacking something. When everything comes together perfectly, it is about entertaining the audience from the hearts of all the individuals who make up the unit. A successful show is a team effort.

"Wherever you get to, you didn't get there by yourself." "There is a goal greater than you, or the goal is always greater than the struggle." My experience with Tops in Blue reaffirmed these sayings from my grandmothers. The very same people who were so passionate about their talent as performers would stand on the front line to defend our country. You see, these same soldiers who would literally give their lives for people in this country to have democratic freedom are the same people on the other side of the coin who are passionate about performing, entertaining, and uplifting others by touching their lives in a positive way.

Tops in Blue was a team effort 24/7. We traveled on the same buses, the same planes, and we had to learn how to live with each other outside of ourselves. You can't lose yourself in the middle of being part of this family. And, by the same token, you must figure out how to make the "real" you work in this tight team structure. It's all about finding balance.

TEAM BUILDING

WITHIN corporate organizations, I speak to employees and all management levels about increasing productivity based on relationships, commitment, and passion. The topics I present are about productive interoffice and interpersonal relationships. They are about healthy communication skills that fall under the umbrella of team building.

From the day we were born, there has been a team in place to help us succeed. We didn't get to where we are today by ourselves. I challenge you to name any measurable progress or success you've had where there was absolutely no contributing factors from anyone or anything outside yourself. It's not possible! As my grandmother drilled into me: "You didn't do it alone – be grateful to others and let them know they touched your life." We don't accomplish anything in this world alone: whatever happens is the result of the whole tapestry of one's life with all the weavings of individual threads from one another. Let's remember every day to be grateful and say "thank you" to those who have helped us along our way. Let's not just mentally thank them, but let them know in writing or verbally and through our actions.

I CAN'T— YET

I believe if something feels good, do not just do it, but do it big. If something doesn't feel good, learn. Learn from it, because it obviously has a purpose or it wouldn't be in your life. Let your stumbling block be your stepping-stone and know that when something is a struggle the only way out of it is all the way in.

You only have one life—live it in peace, live it in truth, live it in love. Be happy, stay fit and always look to the future. Don't limit yourself. Always take a positive attitude by saying, "I can't do that yet." That's a good practice in other areas of your life. In the decision making process you can ask yourself: what am I waiting for, and, how is this working for me? Don't say "can't," say "I can't—yet," and your next subconscious thought is, "But I will." Elise Reese, a client in 2008, wrote me a gratifying letter:

"When you first took me on as your client, your first words to me were: 'Quitting is not an option!!!' Over the course of eleven months, you have reiterated that mantra, coupled with other phrases such as 'the body doesn't quit, the mind quits,' 'always finish stronger than you start,' 'you can do anything for thirty seconds,' and many other positive anecdotes that have become a part of my everyday living! Pepper, you continue to stretch me beyond my initial chronic, physical illness and mental boundaries, limitations and capabilities to health! To say thank you isn't enough."

ON LEADERSHIP

WE are all leaders in some sense. Before we are leaders, success is all about growing ourselves. When we become a leader, success is all about growing others. If you have children or someone under your care, you are a leader. However, in the business world, everyone who directs or supervises isn't necessarily a leader. We can take an emblem off a Mercedes and put it on a Volkswagen, but that doesn't make it a Mercedes; underneath it is still a Volkswagen. The moral here is that the title we hold doesn't make us an effective leader.

One of the first things I share with executives is that being a successful leader is not about them. Leadership is about developing other people. The role of the leader, just like that of the parent, is to give those we are leading a foundation to build upon. In other words, give them the tools to be successful; give them information that supports their spirit, their passion, their talents, and give them permission to be who they truly are. This gives them the wings to soar, not only in the workplace but in their personal life as well.

It doesn't matter whether I am giving executive workshops or addressing a small group, I explain that being an effective leader is directing people so they are empowered. We may be well educated and experienced, but as leaders we need to have the talent, skills, and ability, to make people want to hear our message and risk change by following it. When I say follow, that doesn't mean we're in the front like the drum major or the Pied Piper. Sometimes the leadership of empowering others, acknowledging and exposing their strengths to them, is leading from behind and then getting out of the way to let them soar.

Leaders make others feel important and special. People tend to follow those who make them feel good about themselves. Like artistry, leadership is not what we see or feel but what we make others see and feel.

Leadership that inspires hope and confidence is essential. To inspire means to fill with spirit. Spirit equates to the energy of life. This is often what is lacking and most needed in our lives. When I'm most effective, I am not motivating individuals, I am empowering them.

INSPIRATION

THE circle of inspiration: the lives we inspire, inspire us.

Martial arts teach that the student becomes the teacher, who becomes the student, who becomes the teacher, in a perpetual circle. The lives we touch inspire us as we inspire them.

I don't care what corner of the world we are living in or under what situation or environment—we can still find inspiration and be inspired by others. For instance, I was touched by a gift I was given in Brazil on a trip to work with homeless kids. I met a 90-year-old woman who gave me a rosary. She went to her Bible and took the rosary out, saying it was given to her by her mother. She kept the rosary her entire life and insisted I take it, because she felt Spirit instructing her that day to give it to me.

The incident speaks to how Universal Spirit works. Spirit had set up that situation for me to be there on purpose at that moment to meet this woman. This woman had NOTHING, yet she shared with me. When we say we have nothing, we don't know what nothing means. She inspired me by her giving, and this experience will stay with me for the rest of my life. I was the only one she insisted on having the rosary. My part in that was to say "thank you" and allow her to give what was Spirit-directed. She also told me some stories that illustrated the miracles she had witnessed in her life, in her own home.

I am humbled by the unsolicited e-mails students send me sharing their experiences in my classes and how they have been inspired. The road of inspiration goes both ways: students are inspired by me and, in turn, I am inspired by them. I can't fully express my soul's gratitude knowing I have touched someone's life. Their responses are the gifts I treasure, not because they could feed my ego, but because students have let me know I have contributed to their lives in a positive, meaningful way, and they have taken the time to share that with me.

One year, I spent six months surviving a very traumatic knee surgery. Two months after the doctors released me from the hospital I was conducting training at the Zumba convention. Part of my presentation was slotted in the section "Be an Inspiration." The experiences during my recovery took me to another level and my presentation was about this journey.

"Be an Inspiration" is about things I have experienced in my life. The impact of the lessons, the miracle moments of the journey, are so valuable for where I'm going. They can be just as impactful for others and where they are going. My purpose is to explain that it is not what happens to us, it is what we do with what happens to us that is most important. In this case, I was able to use my intense medical journey to discuss how the goal is always greater than the struggle.

THE BEAR AND THE HONEY

IN my talk, "The Universe—Your Inspiration," I reference the fable "The Bear and the Honey." The bear is an image of our personal life and needs.

A bear is running around, living its bear life, hungry for honey. Suddenly he spies a beehive up in a tree. What is it that the bear needs that only honey can provide? Why is it that he is focused on the honey regardless of the dangers of the beehive? The answer is simple—in spite of what the bear has attained in life, the honey pot is his ultimate rainbow.

Somewhere in our mind, we all have an ultimate rainbow, whatever that rainbow is. Whether it's owning our own business, becoming a rock star, raising a family, or going to heaven, we all have a rainbow. What the rainbow offers, what it is or is a symbol of, is created in our own thoughts and imagination. The question becomes: where in this entire universe is our ultimate rainbow located; what challenges are we prepared to go through to obtain our rainbow?

So, our bear finds a tree with the hive. Now he is faced with the work of obtaining the honey. He has to put in the work to achieve his goal. How badly does he want the honey?

At the bottom of the tree looking up, he can say to himself, "I have to climb the tree. That honey pot is way too high. It's more work than I thought, and it isn't worth the effort." So, he gives up his rainbow and ambles away. Or the bear realizes that the value of his ultimate rainbow is the most important thing in his life and starts climbing the tree.

After he's climbed the trunk, he must go out on a limb. He thinks, "I see the honey, it's within reach, but now there's another risk. I've got to go out on that skinny branch to retrieve it. The branch could break, and I'd fall far to the ground. Is the honey worth the risk to obtain it?"

This is synonymous with our life. We all want things, but they come with a price, with sacrifices and efforts to achieve them. There's no free lunch, not even for our bear.

The bear decides to risk the branch not holding his weight and goes out on the limb. However, it's not time for him to celebrate quite yet—there's a new danger and challenge. There are bees flying around protecting the hive. He now has to successfully retrieve the hive in spite of the bees and the possibility of being badly stung. He gets the honey, because he reaches for the hive and is well protected by the naturally heavy fur he was gifted with by nature. After he has the honey, he faces the challenge of getting back down the tree. Only then when he gets down and to his cave can he enjoy the honey—the fruits of his courage and labor.

Soon he has eaten all the honey, and he must weigh the risks versus the benefits of repeating the process. He does this by answering the question: what's the goal and at what cost? Then he can make the best choice for himself and his situation.

This is one of the stories I use to help us reflect on the questions: What is our ultimate rainbow? What's it going to take to achieve it? What are the costs? What are the sacrifices, work and risks we are willing to take to achieve our rainbow? After we've reached our goal, then what?

EMPOWERMENT

THE first step in empowering someone is listening and then speaking from the heart. I do this by sharing my own journey and using my experiences as examples to show people that change and growth are not only possible but are available and can be theirs.

In the corporate setting, I ask participants to reflect on their life by answering questions such as: is your job what you do or who you are, are you invested in it completely and does it bring you joy, is it something you'd rather be doing than eating? I ask participants to consider whether they can't see themselves doing anything else, or if their job is something that fills the time between 9-5 and they can't wait to retire.

Leadership in a formal way is not for everyone, but everyone is a leader in some aspect of their life. Whatever we do, if it is providing a service and we are good at it and it is feeding the nucleus of our soul, if we're calm with it and we're at peace with it, then it is healthy. However, when work is stressing us out, giving us heart problems, and is taking over our life in an unhealthy way, we are out of balance. We are not managing life well. If it's so demanding on us, it is fear-based—it is literally killing us, and if we are afraid to leave, then our job owns us. Our life is consumed by it in a toxic way.

A task without joy – whether that lack of joy is due to the people involved or the task itself – is drudgery. Have confidence that serving in the capacity of a leader will be one of the best educational experiences we'll ever have. It teaches us a great deal about ourselves and others.

FINDING OUR PASSION

LEADERSHIP can be an opportunity to find our passion. Passion here is defined as a positive, intense feeling that we experience for something that is profoundly meaningful for us as an individual—it has nothing to do with how much money we make. The pursuit of whatever we are passionate about cannot be separated from who we are. A job is what we have; a career is what we have. Our passion is at the core of our being, and we can never be separated from it.

Leadership, whether paid and part of our job, or in a volunteer capacity, or as head of a household, gives us an opportunity to share our passion and induce change in ourselves, and help others do the same.

CHAPTER 5

Darkness and Despair

HOW old does a guy get before he finally escapes the ghosts of his past?

There is a difference between Pepper Von and Billy Von Veal. I never want some of Billy's experiences to spill over into my life as a part of Pepper. I don't want the pain of my childhood to come into my adult life. I know how the peaks and valleys of my human activity have played out. I've lived them and they make sense, but when parts of Billy's experiences have spilled over into Pepper's, they have created chaos. I know the purpose of Billy's experiences and I'm thankful for the lessons which I carry with me. I can acknowledge the vision of where they are taking me—what worked and what didn't work and what doesn't work today. But I don't want parts of those two life experiences to mix. Certain things belong to Billy Von Veal, not Pepper Von, and I don't need to dwell on them. When they accidently drift over, they come with a lot of pain and dysfunction.

Part of my survival mechanism growing up was in creating this other individual, Pepper. This was a matter of self-survival. My biggest, unconscious panic was the act of waking up. In a nightmare, you may be tossing and turning, maybe talking in your sleep, but the moment you wake up that's when you realize your heart is jumping out of your chest and you're in a mode of extreme panic. You fear going back to sleep, because you don't want to put yourself back in the nightmare experience both physically and psychologically.

For millions of people, our childhood traumas and the cancer of those moments or events filter into our real lives, regardless of how hard we fight them, regardless of how many self-help books we read, and regardless of how often we go to church, or how many meetings we attend. The experience of a dysfunction literally goes into the cells of your hard drive. It may be different for others, but dysfunctions for me result in depression that has come up periodically in the course of my life.

DEPRESSION

IF you've never experienced depression, it is a feeling of sadness, discouragement, of being lonely, or being alone when surrounded by others. Depression does not honor status and material things—it affects the rich and poor, the famous and unknown alike, and the positive person as well as the person who usually sees the glass as half empty. There is no logical reason to feel trapped in something intangible that's dragging you down, but you do and can't seem to help yourself out of the funk. These are painful and miserable feelings.

Sometimes, counseling helps reduce the experience of depression and can help you deal with it, but cannot cure the situation that has made you depressed. Managing it is one thing; compartmentalizing it is another. But just as with any addiction, the dysfunction is never not there.

As a positive adult, I had what I thought were the tools to cope. I acknowledged the dysfunction, but it didn't feel really painful. When you compare your dysfunction and how you are handling it with other people's and what they are dealing with, your problem doesn't look so bad. That's when you think you've successfully dealt with the dysfunction. But it is still there. For me, it was only when both the tools and the pain came together that a turnaround became possible and my healing began.

The scary part of depression is you are one of the lucky ones if you make it to experience the success of what the experience is all about. Still, it is a never-ending process. For me and my character and the person I am, I would rather hurt myself ten times than hurt one person one time either accidently or on purpose. I faced my dysfunction when I realized I hurt other people. That's what I couldn't take—the guilt and shame. Innocently hurting people was not my intention. In that moment, I prayed I would never be in that place again.

What was so difficult for me was the fact that I was way down the road of denial. I was in the middle of the parade only to look back and realize I had sleepwalked through the experience, almost to the point where I was emotionally divorced from the traumatic event that caused such pain. I remembered it but didn't realize it literally had me on the edge of destruction several times.

Often our mind and emotions shut down until we are able to work with such experiences. We have this built-in part of us that won't let us look at these dark issues until we have the strength to address them and not before, because they could destroy us. We need to acquire the tools before we can deal with the events and emotions. I didn't associate the experiences I had at age ten with the behavior of just "survival." I didn't link these together. I looked at the outcome of a traumatic experience and did not have the tools to work through it towards healing. I could have committed suicide because I just wanted the pain to end.

HELPFUL PROGRAMS

WHEN you reach a certain level, there are two options: revert back to shutting down, which takes you into another cycle of depression and you consider suicide, or move forward, no matter how painful it appears, into new programming. I was desperate not to carry all that guilt or all that shame of my childhood further into my adult life. I dove into programs like I was Superman. It didn't matter whether it was eating disorders, sexual dysfunction, alcoholism, chemical abuse—if there was a program anywhere, I went to the meetings. I didn't care what the program was; the information was the important thing. I found all the teachings the same. I was at more AA meetings than anyone who was an alcoholic. I couldn't go to those meetings enough. It was strange when I was talking to people, because I've never had a drink in my life! My sincerity and sensitivity were totally present, so no one had a problem with my being in attendance.

Statements from the AA program brought ideals to the surface and validated them for me. The program, in essence, says that once you have the knowledge and tools, you make these more applicable in your life by paying it forward. Once you are aware of the principles, you make a commitment to follow them. As you get further along in applying the principles, following them becomes automatic.

For me, the AA program was a way of combining separate beliefs I held by bringing things together into a packaged unit. For example, the saying: "See God in people, places and things" is simply put, but encompasses everything. If I choose to see God in people, places and things, there is only one way—there are no exceptions. This principle streamlines our responses in life. Another saying, "We are spiritual beings having a human experience," put life into perspective for me. Living your life forward, being of service, and caring about the safety and success of others are the important ideals. You can only be of service or care for others by acting outside of your own self-interest.

I had to do something to save myself, so the meetings became my life. AA and its 12-Step Program was the path I took to get the information I needed to change my life. Others may receive the messages and tools through religion or different spiritual practices. No one single path is effective for everyone.

Another time I was in the throes of depression, I'd gone to Southern California to an intense program and found myself sitting at the end of the bay in my car, looking at all the water, thinking that if I floored this car right now, I'd be in the ocean and the pain would end. I'd have peace because the space I was in didn't feel good.

At that moment, I felt the pain was bigger than my life. When you are in the throes of depression it's as if something takes over in your mind, saying you don't have to keep dealing with all this grief, you can end the pain. You play all those old experiences in your mind; and there are moments when I still do that. I don't know why I'm still here, because there were times I can pinpoint throughout my life where things could have gone either way, where one second further in a certain direction, I would have died.

I hope that sharing the experience I had in the car can be valuable to others. Someone else could have those suicidal thoughts where there were no drugs or alcohol in their system. It is a matter of depression. Depression can be all-encompassing, and it takes over your life—almost like a case of possession. If people haven't wrestled with depression, they don't understand how overpowering it can be, even for the strongest people. It can happen to anyone at any time. Prescribing drugs is not the answer; the side effects usually compound or mask the problem.

We hear about teenage suicides all the time. In our society, we tend to think suicidal thoughts are for teenagers who are at that point of trying to figure out life. Or maybe we think of it occurring in people like police officers and soldiers who experience extreme mental trauma like PTSD. On the news we don't hear about everyday people. When a professional athlete comes out and says, "I was raped at age seven and I suffer from depression, we are shocked. But we don't relate that these types of situations happen to real people, people we know. Yet they do.

GIFTS IN DISGUISE

WE can transcend our traumas by recognizing that what appear as problems are really gifts in disguise. Every pain we suffer carries within it the seeds of a greater opportunity. Many times, the greatest problems of our lives turn out to be the biggest blessings, because these problems challenge us to be better, grow stronger and reach farther. Most often, we come through difficult times having changed in ways we never would have without the experience. If we miss the gift inside our pain and resort to blaming or self-pity, we simply suffer and can suffer to the point where depression takes over our lives and makes decisions for us.

If we have the courage to recognize our problems as spiritual signposts that carry messages for us, then we can gratefully accept the gift and transmute it into a lesson of love. Love is a healing force. Just as every problem proposes its own solution, every pain always contains the exact amount of love inside to soothe its own sting. It takes courage to live in this way, with this attitude.

I have had to work through the trauma of my childhood rape. Others may still have their own traumas to work through. Because we are all human, there may be a moment when sharing my experience can help others. I have compassion and understand their pain. We all have character defects and challenges, and moving through them with a spiritual solution brings acceptance and growth.

Continually I carry that childhood experience and others with me, and every decade or so, depression pops up. Every time I read about depression, see something on television, or speak to someone, it sounds like (at least the way it is stated) they blamed that childhood experience on their own behavior. I can identify with this feeling but that does not make it acceptable or right. One of the programs I attended in Los Angeles had me write a letter to my ten-year-old self. Even though I didn't blame him because he wasn't the adult, I still never allowed him to forgive himself. That was huge! I had to forgive and love myself. I had to believe this—not just in words, but deep down in the core of my being, down to my DNA.

Today, because I am called to do grief counseling, I understand why I was supposed to experience all those dysfunctional feelings and wrestle with depression. With any kind of addiction or dysfunction, you can't successfully counsel people if you haven't personally been there.

PERSONAL RESPONSIBILITY

I am not a person who does well in the victim role and having no control over myself. My character doesn't do well in that kind of situation. This is another reason I don't drink. Spiritually, my first responsibility is to be in control of myself at all times, being aware and responsible for my actions. To do that, all my faculties must be operating at their highest potential. Regardless of the outcome, I hold myself responsible for my actions. I want to be able to credit myself with the success of the outcome or the lesson from it. Either way, it is my choice.

BURGLARY

WE were getting ready for a show and I called a rehearsal of my dance company, Bodytalks. We were using a rented studio. The rehearsal space was a one-story home that had been converted into a studio. It was an older building without air conditioning. From the front door, you could see through the lobby into the studio and its mirrors. We were having night rehearsals, because they had to be after we got off work, school, or in my case, when I finished teaching at the college. The group would get there before I did. Usually when I pulled up, I would see cars parked along the street, hear music, and could see people milling around. When I got there this particular night there were cars parked but no sound. The door was closed, and the night was warm. There was no music, no ambience, so the energy felt strange.

I got the feeling that something was off. But my mind was on the rehearsal—show up, get in, get going—so my mind's autopilot continued. When I opened the door, I couldn't see the dancers. Cars were outside, but there were no people! I took a couple of steps in and a gun was put in my face. The person wore a ski mask and was dressed in black. He said, "Don't try to be a hero, or you'll die tonight."

I thought he was alone, but it turned out there were two more men. At this point I'm thinking, "Where are the dancers?" I was taken into the main dance room, and everyone was lying face down on the floor. Some people were also lying on the floor in the dressing room in the back.

The thugs were aggressive with everyone to intimidate us. I think the initial goal of the criminals was to rob everyone and their cars—take the purses and quickly go through the cars. It evolved into a lot more physically aggressive behavior when they discovered the power they held. Once they saw there were only a few males, and all these girls dressed as dancers, and realized they had full power and control of the situation, it went to their heads.

I was lying face down on the dance floor, but I could hear what was going on, and there was nothing I could do. It was extremely difficult for me, with two black belts in martial arts, to find myself powerless, not being able to do anything to save anyone from harm, and for all of us to be so vulnerable. We were all held at gunpoint, so there was never a question of me doing something to "save" us.

It was a senseless, criminal activity—a robbery and sexual assault. One held the gun on us while one was sexually assaulting some of the girls. As the director, I placed myself responsible for the safety of the troupe. Yet, I could do nothing but allow the scene to play out. I chose not to do anything to make the situation worse and get anyone killed. At this point, the thugs didn't show any fear, and there was nothing and no one to stop their aggressive behavior.

As a martial artist, I was trained to be in charge of my energy, my movements, my choices. Being unable to do anything in this situation was a really dark hole to be in. My compassion, just like with our own children, was with my troupe, and I experienced their pain heavier than my own. I thought more of what everyone else was going through in that moment.

We were nowhere near the lobby or the door, so we couldn't see when they came and went. One took all the keys and went outside to go through the cars. Another held a gun on us while the other one was in the other room. There was a gun on us at all times. In the end, as we laid face down, we were told not to move. "If anyone moves, we'll kill you. Don't make any sound."

I couldn't tell if they were still standing over us or were in the lobby watching. I couldn't hear them or trust they were not standing in the lobby just waiting for one of us to make a move. I couldn't hear anything except crying. It felt like hours but was probably minutes. The quiet reminded me of being on the battlefield when the bombing has stopped, and the guns are silent, and you hear the moaning of the wounded—all the residual sounds from the activity of the tragedy. After a while all my senses told me they couldn't possibly still be there—there was no rustling about, no sound of them, nothing. I had no idea how much time had passed or if they were outside the building waiting for us. I took a chance, looked around, got up, and they were gone. Everything after that was following procedure—calling the police, reporting the crime with each of us giving a statement.

Burglary-based sexual assault was not as widespread in 1987. It was a dramatic event—that's not to say it wouldn't be now. The impact, as well as the event itself to those involved, is still horrific. Today people have more mismanaged emotional pain, so their behavior is more destructive. We have younger, more aggressive criminals with less remorse and the use of guns in a crime is more prevalent than it was in the '80s.

One of the girls who was there was able to identify an assailant, and the police were able to catch two of them. We did have to go to court to testify. The Bodytalks troupe didn't break up over it—we didn't fall apart as a performing dance company. It was near to the time Step 1 was opening, so we didn't rehearse at that location again.

RESIDUAL EFFECT

WITH a traumatic event, there is always a certain residual effect. If you drive down a particular street and turn on a certain corner where you were involved in a head-on collision, it doesn't matter if the buildings that were there have been torn down and a new high rise built, there is a little tweaking that goes on inside of you. Even now when I drive past the area in which the robbery occurred, though the building has changed, I feel a pull. Today, 27 years later, Mary Wright, my business partner, and I are extremely cautious about the doors to the studio being locked when crews are in rehearsing and it is late at night.

The residual effect doesn't mean you can't or don't heal. You want the experience erased, because you've already worked through it, but that residual memory of the event is still there. Certain sounds can trigger memories. Certain aromas, or certain songs take you immediately back to that moment. It is strange how I see one of the dancers a couple of times a week, I see her husband at least once a week, their daughters took lessons at Step 1 until college age, but I don't see that moment of the robbery when I look at her. We see each other in a healthy environment, in a healthy life, healed individuals, not as victims of that event. Yet, if we were to walk, hand and hand, over to the area, we would experience the pain of the burglary again.

What was going through me when I was lying there? Part of it was about me not being able to control the situation. The major part was about what the others were going through—that's what was piercing my heart. In my head, my martial arts training was running: even though I can't control or do anything, what should I be paying attention to? From this event I had to learn not to assume guilt for something I had no control over. I realized a long time after the incident that forgiving myself, and forgiving everyone else, even the perpetrators of the crime, was the only way I could heal.

NEAR DROWNING

I don't know where my dad got the idea to enlist in the Navy—maybe he swam in the Mississippi River. But I didn't swim in the Mississippi and we weren't allowed in the white, public swimming pool. We had no black swimming pool in the neighborhood, so I was no friend of water. I remember when I was young, my Aunt Saint in Ohio tried to give me swim lessons, but they didn't stick with me. I was an adult before I would learn to swim.

While stationed in Arizona, a group of us were planning on the simple fun of tubing in a canal. It didn't cross my mind that I didn't know how to swim. We were each in an inner tube in fast-moving water and I capsized—I completely flipped. I remember that moment of consciously knowing I was in trouble. I was heavily into martial arts at the time, and my martial arts training ran through my mind. That training said, "Be calm; then you can see the whole situation more clearly in spite of the threat."

I knew all I had to do was follow the current and make my way to the side as opposed to going crossways against the current. I followed the flow of the water. The sides of the canal were all concrete, angled up at a steep 45 degrees with the first three or four feet covered in slippery algae. I remember trying to reach up for a metal beam as it went across the canal, but the current was too fast, and I couldn't grab it. It was like trying to grab a pole from the window of a car going 30 miles per hour—just not possible. That's when I knew I was really in trouble—I couldn't get out, and the canal went on and on for miles. The one thing you learn in any drowning or potential drowning situation is that panic will kill you. Even if there is a way to escape, panic will kill you. That's when I surrendered to God.

A member of the group was instrumental in saving me. He was able to reach into the water and grab me. I don't remember how —I was unconscious by that time. I don't remember the paramedics. I remember waking up in the ambulance on the way to the hospital, but I don't remember the incident itself.

I was in my early 20s, and throughout my life I have, at times, kept God and my angel ancestors busy with some dangerous life experiences. This was one of those times. Upon reflection I thought to myself, "I must have a pretty important task if I'm still here."

SCUBA DIVING

AT one time, I had an agent in New York who was booking most of my media appearances, on-air events and commercial work. I was a fitness athlete. An opportunity came up having to do with promoting and protecting ocean life and a reef. The final script called for a challenge between fitness athletes and bodybuilders. My agent was excited about this project and signed the contract. I envisioned it being like a telethon, performing in an aquarium with us competing in front of a tank to raise money: "Do this workout with me… call and make your pledge." It turned out the competition was going to be in the Caribbean—in the ocean!

My agent said, "The challenge will be full-on in real water doing certain activities—like an obstacle course."

"Okay, I resign!" I said.

"I don't play in the water. I'm not a swimmer. I don't go in the water," I reiterated.

She said, "They've only chosen ten people out of all the fitness personalities in the United States, and you're one of them—this is a great opportunity for you. It will be the top five fitness personalities and the top five bodybuilding personalities competing against each other. It's the aerobically fit versus the strong muscles guys."

"So, how does this work? I'm not getting in the water, and you refuse to retract the contract?"

She said, "You're going to learn how to swim!"

Hmm... At that time I didn't have any experience swimming— none! I had no plans of ever purposefully being in the ocean or in the water thanks to my previous canal experience.

She said, "You take some classes, and you learn to be comfortable in the water. We'll pay for all your lessons."

Well, I thought, I may as well do it—if all else fails, I'll learn how to swim.

At 40-something, I signed up to take lessons at the YMCA. They didn't have enough adults for a class, so I had to be in the beginning kids class! When I walked out of the men's locker room the first day, a little girl said, "You don't know how to swim?"

I said, "No."

And she said with an attitude, "But you're a grown-up."

She could not believe an adult didn't know how to swim. I thought, "Smart kid, I should crush you right now!"

Swimming was a new experience, like learning to walk. The instructor was amazing. I got in the water waist deep, and she said, "Everyone put your face in the water. "

Hmmm... That wasn't good; I knew you couldn't breathe underwater. I did it for a nanosecond, wiped my face off as though I'd done it in ten feet of water, and thought I'd really done something huge.

To me, the only way out is all the way in. I rationalized if I'm going to fulfill my contract, I'm going to take swim lessons and, knowing myself, I'm going to be aggressive about practicing. I found a health-club pool where I could practice what I was learning when I had a break during the day. I joined the club only for that reason.

That's the way things started. Then I found out I needed to learn to function under the water! A friend's husband had a buddy who taught scuba diving. I was told you didn't need to know how to swim to dive, so I signed up to take dive lessons at the same time I was learning to swim.

Okay, I thought, how can it be that you don't need to know how to swim to dive? I was so naïve. I wanted to believe it was true but of course it turned out to be a lie!

After my first swim lesson I had my first dive class that evening. What I did not know was that Steve, the diving instructor, was a former Navy SEAL! Well, that says a whole lot about how he trains people. He was a very aggressive and demanding instructor because that's the way they do things in SEAL training.

For starters, SEAL training is ruthless. It involves endless miles of running in the wet sand while wearing boots (28 minutes for four-mile runs), timed obstacle courses, open-water swims (two miles in 75 minutes) in the 60-degree temperature of the Pacific Ocean, scuba training involving taking off, repairing and reassembling gear while submerged with no oxygen supply, "drown proofing," where you are dropped into a deep pool with both hands and legs bound, retrieving objects from the bottom of the pool with your teeth, plus other torturous trials of combat and weaponry. It is tough to get through SEAL training. Only the best survive and graduate, but that's their approach, and they get results. I knew none of this starting the dive class.

I can't swim. The first night of dive class, Steve blows his whistle and says, "Everyone get in the water and do 12 laps up and back!"

Everyone gets in the shallow end and takes off swimming, except me. I'm standing up there, looking at him while he's looking at me, looking at him! He says, "What's your problem?"

"I'm not going in there. I can't swim." He thinks I'm being defiant. "I'm telling you, I can't swim, so I'm not going down there to the deep end."

This drill should have taken about 15 minutes. Steve blows his whistle and says, "Everyone has to keep swimming until Pepper has done 12 laps."

No peer pressure! The others are shouting, "Get your ass in the water!" They are tired and really upset, thinking it's not their problem but they are being punished! And finally, I talked to myself and said,

"I've got to get down there."

After only one swim lesson, I don't know anything about swimming yet. I get in the water, and from cartoons and watching others, I think all I've got to do is move my arms and legs and turn my head from side to side (not knowing anything about breathing techniques—how you blow out in the water and inhale when your head is on its side). I'm following the markings on the side of the pool. I'm okay at five feet. I can still stand up and keep my head above water. I'm good. The moment I saw seven feet, it was all over. I panicked—I couldn't stand up. I couldn't reach the bottom, and I freaked out. I make my way to the side of the pool. There's a little trench, and I'm literally throwing up. Everyone around me is concerned, asking if I was okay, calling for Steve.

Steve doesn't move. He didn't jump in and check on me or anything. He's still standing in three feet of water and yells at me, "God-damn it! Quit drinking all of our water!"

Being a Taurus my horns went up, and I was very angry that he could be that careless with my life. Needless to say, he and I got off to a bad start. I'm supposed to trust him to get me through this course, and I told him I couldn't swim, and he reacts as if I am being defiant! That was my first night! Talk about trauma, and I was supposed to come back for more? Another night and another night?

The next day, I told my swimming instructor at the Y that I was under contract to do this dive competition and about my experience the previous night where I'd almost died. I told her, "I'm on a time-line—I've got this contract, and these are my goals."

She started giving me other skills to practice ahead of the class that were a bit more progressive, like how to float on my back. With her help, I got to the point where I wasn't as afraid to get in the water.

The next night in dive class Steve said to me, "I don't care how you get down there and back, just get down there and back." I could float on my back for a bit, turn over and dog paddle, then float again, so I did get down and back.

We had classroom time that alternated with dive time. In the third class, he said, "We are going to do equipment." We learned how the mouthpiece works, how the oxygen works in class. I'm thinking, "Okay, this is good."

Then he says, "Jump into the bottom at 12 feet, sit on the bottom, take off the equipment, leave it there, and swim on the bottom all the way back to three feet."

I couldn't do it! It was a nightmare. In a TV sitcom, it could be hilarious, but in my reality, it was a disaster in the making. I'm thinking this guy is getting crazier by the day. This guy should be on medications. He's not right. My love for him was not growing.

Steve had no sympathy, understanding or tolerance for me. His training was strict—the same way he was trained—so he gave me no latitude. I told myself, "Walk through the fear. Follow his instructions. You can do this." My self-talk helped me make my way through that experience.

In the next class we learned about oxygen, figuring return time, depth, and calculating how much pressure per square inch was being exerted upon you. The next time we were in the water, Steve instructed us to take our equipment, stand on the side of the pool, throw it in the water and watch it sink. He then instructed us to jump in and, no matter how long it took, put the equipment on while we were on the bottom. While I'm still just starting to learn to swim he was having us perform survival drills.

In another lesson, Steve had us sit on the bottom of the pool with our equipment while we were blindfolded, because when you dive, it is dark down in the water. At the time I didn't understand that these are survival skills. At this point for me, it is about overcoming my phobias. All I wanted to do is learn how to dive. I'm not trying to become a Navy SEAL! We're down there, sitting, and we can't see anything, and then all of a sudden, without warning, my air is gone! You're not supposed to panic. I do! I've just exhaled, and now there is nothing to inhale. What do I do? I bolt to the surface! That is a huge mistake. A huge no-no! You are not allowed to do that because, in a real-life situation, you could get the bends and your lungs could explode. That won't happen at 12 feet, but the idea was to practice a survival behavior. My reaction was immediate, so, of course, everyone had to go through all these additional drills, because I had bolted to the surface.

In truth, Steve was embarrassing me to save my life. That was his method. That was the way Navy SEALs were trained, and it was evidence-based training, leading to success. I just happened to be the one who could not control my reaction. The others knew there was still air in their lungs; your lungs can expand even more with residual air, even though you don't suck in more air. I didn't understand that. In my mind, there was air or the absence of air—nothing in between.

Everything about swimming and diving was unfamiliar, but I stayed in. What was being demanded of me was unfamiliar. Everything about the situation was unfamiliar to me—a new language—but I knew my reactions were all based on fear. I was conscious enough to know that fear-based experiences are not as real as I magnified them to be in my mind. The events were real, but the threats were not real. I took control of myself, did my Nine Ds solution-based, success techniques – which we will get to later – and I made it through the lessons.

Throughout the training I contemplated murdering Steve. It was a running gag: "I know people. I could get Steve bumped off." I had no love for that man whatsoever, and he didn't demonstrate any for me. We didn't care. We were there for a reason, we didn't have to like each other, and we didn't. In the end, we became amazing friends, because the outcome was a reflection of my success in other areas of my life. However, at the time, while we may have grudgingly respected each other, we didn't like each other.

The final dive was in Monterey Bay. My business partner at Step 1, Mary Wright, and friend, Janice Mitchell, came out to support me. I did the dive with Janice as my dive partner. The evening before the dive, Steve stood on a rock overlooking the ocean and saw a storm coming in. The next day, the storm arrived with gale-force winds! Janice asked, "Steve are we still going to dive?" "Yeah, we're going in" was his reply.

Of course, Steve would say that—he was a Navy SEAL! The weather was bad, the water choppy—certainly not the ideal situation for a dive. We had several skills or drills to perform to complete the dive. One involved the use of a compass to navigate. Janice and I had to lock arms to stay together to use the compass to get back to the beach. Surfacing at the end, we had to crawl out rather than roll out, because the waves were too strong. First, Janice surfaced and crawled out, and I took off her fins and equipment. Then I crawled out, and she did the same for me.

Ultimately, I was fine, and I performed as one of the best in the class. I was on my way to fulfilling the contract. In six weeks I went from not knowing how to swim—taking swim lessons with little kids, and doing everything wrong in the diving pool—to being the safety diver for my entire team in the ocean during the competition.

THE CONTEST

DURING the ESPN contests, the two teams competed in several challenges. One event called for us to canoe out in the ocean, dive in, swim to a buoy, ring a bell, and then use lifesaving techniques to drag another team member back. Another challenge was to dive down and retrieve things, like in a scavenger hunt. I was the safety diver on the team—almost like a lifeguard. I was assigned the duty of making sure everyone was safe in the water, because, ironically, I'd had the best previous diving training. Our crew won the contest.

Upon reflection, all the life experiences and the martial arts training were instrumental to my success in that journey. I learned a lot about walking through fear, about not letting fear decide for me how successful I was going to be. My life approach is, "The only way out is all the way in." I started far behind in the diving class because I was the least experienced, and ended up at the top of the class because of my willingness not only to succeed but to super-succeed.

FEAR-BASED LIVING

FEAR is expensive—mentally, emotionally, spiritually and physically. Be bold, be brave!

FEAR is False Evidence Appearing Real. Fear has many causes. It can be caused from a lack of willingness to try: "I've never done it before—I might not be good at it and embarrass myself." Or, "I'm afraid of failing." No one knows what it's like to live without fear; we have to determine what we are afraid of. Too many of us count ourselves out before we even give ourselves a chance.

The word fear doesn't have a home in my perception. I don't use the phrase "fear of failure" these days, because I have taught myself I can't fail. Fear of failure to me is not trusting that I will do the best I can do. When we fear failure, that means we really don't feel we are committed to giving something our best effort.

Doubting ourselves is the same thing. Once we show up to meet a challenge with all we are gifted with in life—our talents and resources—we need prayer to Spirit. We need to ask Spirit, to open our eyes to our talents and be grateful we have been given the opportunity to share our gifts. We need to ask that Spirit is behind us and supports us. Once we go in fully committed, what is there to lose? Don't wait—do it now! The secret is not to wait until we feel we are ready to do something. Our state of readiness is a state of illusion. We are ready when we do it! Waiting is coming from a state of FEAR.

We have doubts, because our ego is at work. As long as we do not recognize how our ego works, how it manifests, and the devious ways in which it hides behind handy excuses to hold us back through fear, we will not be able to master ourselves.

The truth is, we can't possibly lose even if we don't walk away with a medal. How would we live our lives—circumstance to circumstance, event to event, opportunity to opportunity—if we couldn't fail, if it was impossible to fail? This concept dissolves fear. Fear just goes out the window. It's impossible to fail if we have learned something through the opportunity.

Since I have learned these concepts and programmed them into my brain, I don't have a fear of failure because I can't fail. The actor, Will Smith, said he teaches his kids that when you fail, you just have to learn how to fail forward. Instead, what we are taught is that when we fail, we stop or fall backwards to what is safe. The possibility of failure has such a negative connotation now that people pull back in horror. Instead of thinking, "what if I fail?" you could be saying "what if I don't fail?" What does that look like?

We often find people to support our fears and then take their advice. When we take their advice, we dig ourselves into a deeper hole. Failing forward is an interesting idea. It means we learn a lesson, gain knowledge and move on, taking the lesson with us to the next experience. It's natural to have doubts, but we can adopt the attitude of Thomas Edison when he worked to invent the lightbulb: "I have not failed. I've just found 10,000 ways that won't work."

Imagine if, in elementary school, we were taught failing is impossible. What would the world be like? Unfortunately, students are not taught to be creative; education is more focused on producing engineers than imagine-neers. To quote Einstein, "Imagination is more important than knowledge." He felt very strongly that the true sign of intelligence is not knowledge, but imagination. "Logic," he says, "will get you from A to B. Imagination will take you everywhere."

Life is learned through time and experience. I admit there are times when moving through fear is more challenging than others. When I'm in the emergency room with asthma, I'm fighting for a breath, and I don't know if I'm going to live another minute, the opportunity to choose fear is there—it's real. Then I ask myself, "What's available for me to reach out and grab hold of instead?" I always end up with God, but I still get to choose: fear, panic, anxiety and death, or peace, calm and light.

PHOBIAS, ANCHORS AND ELEVATORS

GIVING power to phobias, anchors and elevators can hold us where we are in life. They may feel like a safe place, but they do not contribute to our growth and happiness.

A phobia is a fear, something that is irrational and illogical, which may be the result of a branded experience. A branded experience is something that sticks with us and gives us a license to continue to suffer or to stop our personal growth. It leaves a scar that can be physical, but so often is psychological. Giving too much power to phobias or branded experiences creates fears, which can act as anchors in our lives. We haul the anchors through our lives until we become aware that they are holding us down and we decide to change our behavior.

An elevator can either go down or up. Fear can drive our elevator down, or it can elevate us to a greater success. Some fears can actually elevate our actions. To say, "I don't want to experience that (fill in the blank) again, or I am afraid of ever feeling that (fill in the blank) again," acts as a motivator for change. For example, I may go to the gym to work out because that heart attack didn't work for me and I am dedicated to taking better care of myself— this acts as an elevator going up.

WALKING THROUGH FEAR

I had a branding experience, a near accidental drowning, when I was in the Air Force. It was such a terrifying experience, it left me with a built-in fear, a branding, of water. This was years before the scuba diving fitness challenge came from ESPN.

Initially, when my agent contacted me and I told her emphatically, no, I wasn't going to compete, she had already signed the contract, not knowing of my fears. Arguing with myself, I ultimately felt honor-bound to uphold the commitment made in my name. The process of learning to swim at my age, and with my branded experience, required me to walk my talk of the Nine Ds to success. Following all the steps in the Nine Ds is a lesson in walking through fear and being empowered so that you don't have to go through the rest of your life afraid of something. For me, it was water. In six weeks, I struggled mentally, emotionally, physically and spiritually. I followed the Nine Ds to go from not knowing how to swim to being the safety diver on the team that won the competition. This was a huge accomplishment for me.

As my friend Tru Adams says, "You can't be busy living your dreams if you are busy living your fears." I learned to let my faith be bigger than my fears, knowing there were people in my life to help me succeed.

It is up to us to recognize who our helpers are in each situation and to reach out to them. For me that is humbling. I am always the one others look to for assistance. Yet, it is not for them to guess what my needs are or how they could help. It is up to me to speak up and ask for their support and aid.

CHAPTER 6

Paths to Success

THE NINE DS FORMULA FOR SUCCESS

IF people didn't quit when the going got tough, they would have nothing to regret the rest of their lives.

GETTING TO SUCCESS

The Nine Ds for success are:

DREAM BIG- we create vision of how to accomplish our goals.

DESIRE- we must want something more for ourselves.

DECISION- we make the decision to do something.

DISCIPLINE- we must be willing to sacrifice through focused behavior.

DEDICATION AND COMMITMENT- consistency of action programs the expectancy of success in our minds.

DETERMINATION, CONFIDENCE, AND COURAGE- is pushing through opposing forces and limitations imposed by our own ego.

DIRECTION- involves implementing a plan and following our path.

DO- get it DONE, take action!

DISTRIBUTE- sharing our success and lessons with others.

DESIRE, DECISION, DEDICATION, DISCIPLINE

THE first step in getting to success, or anywhere, is to Dream Big. It's okay to dream and think big in creating the vision of what it is we choose to gain or accomplish. The saying goes, "Aim at heaven, and we get the earth thrown in." To dream about our vision is nice, but we must wake up, live it, and make it real. "If you can dream it, you can achieve it," Walt Disney said. He spoke from experience. His achievements happened because he woke up, worked hard toward his dream and lived it. The second is the Desire for something different. The third is to make the Decision that we're not going to stay where we are.

Decision goes along with the idea that, before we achieve anything, we have to desire something—whatever it is. This goes back to the fable of the Bear and Honey. The next step is to plan. Most think the next step is taking action, but more mental work is required beforehand. Planning begins in making the decision and then Dedicating yourself to do something. To make things happen requires motivation. Motivation is where the visible and invisible merge in what we call creativity. Stay simple—do not complicate things by over-thinking the process. Over-thinking often ruins the plan; second-guessing ourselves allows our egos to get in the way. This easily leads to our twisting things around, making us worry, making us spend endless time planning for every contingency, and making everything much more difficult in our mind than it really is. Find your Direction and implement your plan by following the path you've laid out.

There is a truth: until one is dedicated, there is hesitancy, the chance to draw back, which brings with it ineffectiveness. The lack of dedication kills ideas and plans. But the moment we definitely commit, Spirit moves too. All sorts of things occur to help us that would never have happened otherwise. A whole stream of events come from the decision, bringing unforeseen incidents and material assistance which we could not have dreamed would have come our way. So, as Goethe advises, "Whatever you can do, or dream you can, begin it. Boldness has genius, power and magic in it. Begin it now!"

Confidence enables discipline. The need for Discipline speaks for itself—that's the work, the perseverance to stick with your plan. Discipline leads to success. Just Do It! Get it DONE. This involves a willingness, and the use of elbow grease, to do the work. Be excellent. Have the Determination to push through challenges and opposing forces and the dictates of our ego, remembering that challenges may be placed in our path to test our commitment.

The only difference between try and triumph is a little "umph." The more we increase our output, the closer we get to whatever our goal is. That is, we increase our ability to reach our goal and be successful. If we are pursuing a college degree, the more we study, the more work we put in, the closer we get to our goal. It's the same with sports. The more we run, the faster we get, and the more strategies we have for meeting the goal of winning.

We can't just say, "Oh, I have a destination, and I want to be successful, but I don't seem to be making any progress. I'm not moving forward." A lot of movement doesn't mean progress. The question becomes: Are we putting enough effort into the endeavor to reach our goal? Or are we sabotaging the possibility of being successful by not increasing our output?

ARE YOU READY

THE one who successfully reaches his or her goal is the one who does what's necessary. We don't get buff arms without working out. We don't reach our goal without working for it. This is a conversation I often have when someone complains he or she hasn't reached a certain goal they've set. After explaining the goal, the individual uses the excuse nothing is happening, and the following dialogue often goes like:

Me: Are you ready? If you haven't done something, is it because you aren't ready?
The Person: "I'm here. Doesn't that mean I'm ready?"
Me: "No, showing up signifies your intention, but it doesn't mean you've taken action. Have you started?"
The Person: "No."
Me: "Then you're not ready."
The Person: "Well, how will I know when I'm ready?"
Me: "When you do it!"

WILLINGNESS AND COURAGE

IT takes two things to reach our goals: willingness and courage. Willingness is the trigger that allows us to begin to leave the old. Sometimes we are willing to do what's needed, but we don't have the courage to do it yet. Always take a positive attitude by saying, "I can't do that yet." That's a good practice in all areas of our life. Don't say, "I can't." Say "I can't—yet," and our next subconscious thought is, "But I will."

Courage is defined as the quality of mind or spirit that enables a person to face difficulty, danger, and be in pain without fear. It is the ability to try new things and act with bravery and confidence. When courage is missing, we need to become our own hero. The conversation above continues:

Me: "What is your definition of a hero?"

The Person: "Not being afraid."

Me: "No, in truth, a hero is afraid but does what is required anyway. You think the firemen who went into the buildings on 9/11 weren't afraid? Sure, they were, but they went in anyway. Become your own hero."

The Person: "How do I become my own hero?"

Me: "Do you have what it takes to face this challenge? At what cost? Are you willing to make change or take a risk?

The Person: "Yes, I think so."

Me: "Why?"

The Person: "I think I deserve it."

Me: "Don't think; believe. Because you don't get what you deserve, you get what you believe."

The Person: "Okay, say I believe and still nothing happens."

Me: "Sometimes there are life moves we need to make first, and those can be scary. Are you sabotaging the possibility of being successful? Only you can answer that question. Whatever the answer is may seem scary."

The Person: "I don't know. I'm willing to work hard."

Me: "Do you have courage?"

The Person: "Hmmm…I don't really know. I never thought about that."

Me: "If you are willing and don't have courage, you can pray for courage, but it usually isn't granted. Instead, what comes your way is the opportunity to be courageous! If you lack courage, think, 'I can't yet.' Having willingness and courage comes back to choice. It's your choice to take action or not."

COME TO THE EDGE

"Come to the edge," he said.

"We're comfortable back here," they said.

"Come to the edge," he said.

"We're too busy," they said.

"Come to the edge," he said.

"We're afraid," they said.
"Come to the edge," he said.
"We'll fall," they said.
"Come to the edge," he said.
And slowly, reluctantly, they came.
He pushed them, and they flew.

  - *Guillaume Apollinaire*
    (1880-1918)

THERE is a Divine order to all things. In nature a sequential order exists, so it is for our plans. After we've set our plan in action, we can expect measurable progress in a reasonable time. But we must remain open and flexible. Our plan may take us where we least expect it. However, when doors don't open and we hit the proverbial brick wall, it is time to reflect on the plan and possibly pursue a different path, because when the time is right, the desired results happen without forcing.

Do not interpret "not forcing" to mean "with little effort." Just because something is not happening doesn't mean it never will. It could mean that according to Divine plan, we're not ready for it, even though we think we are. It could be that the timing is off, or something, or someone, or an experience is missing that will contribute to our success.

When true passion is lacking in our spirit, or something doesn't feel right in our gut, then our dream may be an illusion, and when pursued beyond an honest effort, will never happen because something is missing. Then it is time to re-examine our goal. Accept that forcing by investing energy in things that are not meant to happen leads us to frustration and burnout.

DISTRIBUTE

THE last step—and it is a critical part of the process—is to Distribute or share our success, or the lessons learned, with others, whether it's sharing our time, money, resources, teaching, mentoring or speaking. Whatever opportunity presents itself and wherever we are called to serve, we do so by sharing our journey, not from the point of ego, but saying, "If I did it, you can too."

I distribute through public speaking in many different venues, from corporate to athletic trainings, classes at Step 1 and performing. All are ways for me to articulate concepts to people.

I'm very visual, so that's my most effective media in all its different guises. What I share are many of the same concepts my grandmother said to me 50 years ago, but they are new to my audience and participants say, "Wow, that is brilliant. That concept changed my life." Others of you will have different ways to distribute your knowledge. There is no one right answer or one right way to share.

People learn differently, too. Rather than read, I have the ability to listen to someone speak and grab the essentials, filtering out what is extraneous in their words. This is sort of like being able to outline something you've read. When a message comes through dance, music, or some other creative way, my mind forms pictures. These pictures go into my brain—my hard drive. They are always there, so I can reference them when they are appropriate to share with my audience or are needed during my own times of reflection.

Ultimately, we are all a unique speaker system—a megaphone, if you will—distributing from our hearts the knowledge we have gained through our own life experiences. Through selfless sharing, we can lift others up and support them in their growth and development as we communicate our experiences of transformation, lessons learned and success.

The Nine D's of success are available to each of us. And they all lead to the same place—to our own growth. Unless we try to do something beyond what we have already mastered, we will never grow. The first experience is the result of our choices and brings with it a lesson. A repeat of the same experience is because of an un-learned lesson and is a second opportunity to learn it. "The measure of success is not whether you have a tough problem to deal with, but whether it's the same problem you had last year," said John Foster Dulles, U.S. Secretary of State under President Dwight Eisenhower.

LUCK AND SUCCESS

SOME claim the secret of success lies in luck. Luck is one of the words I think should be taken out of the dictionary. Luck is defined as being an event due to chance or a windfall or a fluke. To me, what some call luck is not chance—it's working hard. Therefore, luck doesn't enter into the equation of success. Success often lies in the things we do every day—in consistency of action. Consistency or steadiness brings expectancy—the probability of success or manifestation of our dream. We create luck through manifestations of our thoughts, intentions and actions.

Success is relative and may be referenced as success in the moment, or success over a lifetime. Success is also defined by ten people in ten different ways. A spiritual leader may say you are successful based on your contribution to the world, even if you don't win a prize or come in first.

My definition of success means having a balance across all areas of my life. I can't truly be considered successful in my business life if my personal life is in chaos. The wise person keeps success in perspective and doesn't sell his or her soul to achieve it. There is a lesson in almost everything we do, and getting the lesson is how we move forward. It is how we enrich our spirit—that is success. Successful people are balanced and live in a way that benefits not only themselves but everyone around them.

What the world calls success is, oftentimes, merely celebrity status. Too often success in our culture is based on physical, tangible goals. People who think that if your bank account goes up you are successful, even if you are a miserable human being, are the people who know the price of everything and the value of nothing. They are so poor, all they have is money, and they make money a symbol of their success. They don't understand, or have lost sight of the fact, that friendships, not money, make people happy. Wealth may get in the way of things that matter. It may distract and reduce real happiness.

This isn't to say there's anything wrong with being a millionaire. I am not saying not to enjoy luxuries, that luxuries are horrible things. No, they are not, but what do they mean and at what cost? Where do they take us? Are we taking them too seriously as a means of measuring our success? If it takes us into self-centeredness or ego, then they aren't going to get us into heaven. We can ask ourselves, at the end of life's journey: what defined our success, what were we living for? Part of the lesson for us is to never get so busy making a living that we forget to make a life.

When we can get outside ourselves and not demand life to continue as it has, or is, or what we want it to be, we become open to new experiences. Having invested so much in one direction, we think that investment is going to go to waste if we don't keep going. Whatever we do is never lost—the value is never dead. You think, "I am so close. Am I giving up too soon?" We don't stop and ask ourselves: how's it working for me, and at what cost?

Success is based on our own perception of what we do and how we do it every day. One spiritual leader said the only things that are successful are the things you can take into heaven. Well, that eliminates most tangible things. If we want to set a high standard as to what we consider successful in our life—that being something that will get us into heaven—then whatever is not going to get us into heaven is an illusionary success. That type of success is not real—it is temporary.

RELEVANCE

RELEVANCE is purely subjective, so don't underestimate yours.

In my workshops, I cover relevance. But what does the word relevance mean? Take the automobile for example. We can be told everything about its design and the manufacturing that went into it, but I want to know why it is relevant. I want to know the impact it had on the world of transportation, the impact on daily life. That shows its relevance to me.

In the workshops, I make relevance personal. I begin by talking about the word itself. We live in a world where many people carry the same title. For instance, there are millions and millions of mothers, so my basic question is: In a world where there are millions of mothers, other than carrying the title on a birth certificate, what makes a mother relevant? When we say, "I am a mother", what makes us relevant as a mother? Or makes us relevant as a dancer, or a co-worker? It doesn't matter what you do, at the end of the day, the ultimate question is, what makes us relevant or significant as a human being?

We don't often consider this question of relevance. We don't stop and examine what makes us relevant as a human being – what gives us the privilege of being alive and breathing. Today there is a sense of entitlement, and the answer to our relevancy is often, "Just because."

Just because what? What makes us relevant? Spiritual leaders like the Dalai Lama reference this when they say, "We know what our purpose is that serves us, but what is our purpose of being born that serves others? What makes our birth relevant in the existence of everybody and everything?"

FEEDING OUR PHENOMENA

As Nelson Mandela expresses, "There is no passion to be found in settling for a life that is less than the one you are capable of living." Feeding our phenomena is about enhancing our excellence and relevance. This is very possible; the steps are readily available. When I ask people what makes them relevant as a dancer, a parent, or whatever, it is not for me to tell them anything but for them to reflect and do some soul-searching to uncover their relevance.

We claim labels, yet we don't know what is in our foundation to support those titles. Life hands us challenges, because the Universe believed us when we said, "I am a parent." When we are asked to prove it, it is time to step up and demonstrate what that means. Yet we usually don't think about it in depth. When someone asks us what makes us relevant as a parent, consciously we devise a quick list that goes something like:

- I am a leader
- I am a teacher
- I am a guide
- I am a nurturer
- I am a person with flexibility and strength
- I am a person with sensitivity
- I am grateful that I am willing to be…

I AM

THE phrase, "I AM," is a very powerful statement. It is the creative power of the Universe, for what we put after "I AM" shapes our reality. We can use this power to increase our potential and spirituality. According to Rev. Kevin Ross, the function of I AM is to give power to:

I = Intention
A = Attention
M = Manifestation

Using the phrase "I AM" is like plugging something into electricity; it gains power. I think (I AM); therefore, "I AM". The word "I" is there for a reason. "I" is oneness within ourselves as a unique individual, yet also means oneness with all humanity. We are like the fingers of a hand. Each one is separate with different abilities to contribute to a task, but all are joined on one hand and must work together to accomplish a goal. Once this concept of oneness is cemented in our foundation, the second part is all about serving others.

A CUP OF WATER FROM THE OCEAN

IN the ocean, there are trillions and trillions of life forms that come from that One Source (God). It doesn't matter what that form is—whether it's plant, animal or mineral. If we scoop a cup of water from the ocean and separate it from the Pacific Ocean by taking it to the Atlantic Ocean —it doesn't matter where, we can take it to the moon— the water is still of the ocean. We can't take it far enough to separate it from what it is or from whence it came.

We can have a brilliant idea and say, "I'm going to change the molecular structure of the water. I am going to make sure the molecules are closer together or farther apart." So we freeze the cup of ocean water, causing the molecules to arrange themselves into fixed positions as a solid. Yes, even if the molecules are frozen, the water is still of the ocean. We then decide to separate the molecules by speeding them up turning the water into steam. Even in evaporation, the water is still of the ocean.

The same is true about us. We can never separate who we are from the Source (or God) or from who we are. It is, therefore, vitally important we discover our relevance. The question of relevance applies to whatever we do in our life. Examining our answers to the question of relevance expands the awareness we have of our greatest potential. Whatever our greatest potential is, we are.

We don't get what we deserve. We get what we believe, including those experiences that will help us grow. Remember: Our greatest responsibility in life is to maximize our greatest potential—physically, mentally, emotionally and spiritually.

JOY AND CREATIVITY

CREATIVITY, peace, and joy lift our soul.

I express my joy and creativity through dance, exercise, music, speaking and just being with others. I try to live my life where whatever is inside me paints the outside. Therefore, I pay attention to what I am developing inside. We can fake it for a while, we can lie for a while, but eventually what's inside is going to expose us to the world by showing on the outside.

Dedicated artists put love into their work. My creativity, my creative energies, are in everything I do. Ultimately utilizing the talents I have brings me joy and grants me the opportunity to "pay it forward." These are the vehicles, the mediums, I use.

How do we use what's inside us to reach people? First, just by being who we are—being authentic. We get to meet and interact with people every day. If we are given a gift we learned from someone else, we also have the opportunity to share it with others. Some learn through spoken words, others through the written word, still others through music or movement. I've been given many talents, but they come with the responsibility to share them, not keep them to myself like a miser hoards his gold.

Our goal is to find the courage to share our truth with those closest to us. This type of truth speaking and self-revealing is critical. When you keep your light hidden from yourself and others, no one in the world benefits. It takes courage to live life! We need to have the courage to be our authentic self.

No ray of Light can shine
If severed from its source,
Without my inner Light
I lose my course.
  - Angelus Silesius (c. 1624 – 1677)

The Bible also expresses this concept by instructing us not to hide our light under a bushel. Not sharing our talents is hiding them. We must have the courage to let our light shine by being the best we can be. This can be quietly one-on-one or in a crowd of thousands.

From the wise words of Marianne Williamson:

"Our deepest fear is not that we are inadequate. Our deepest fear is that we are powerful beyond measure. It is our light, not our darkness, that most frightens us. We ask ourselves, 'Who am I to be brilliant, gorgeous, talented, fabulous?' Actually, who are you not to be? You are a child of God. Playing small does not serve the world. There is nothing enlightened about shrinking so that other people won't feel insecure around you. We are all meant to shine, as children do. We were born to make manifest the glory of God that is within us. It's not just in some of us; it's in everyone. And as we let our own light shine, we unconsciously give other people permission to do the same".

Nelson Mandela and Maya Angelou, among others, deliver the same message.

REFLECTION TO PROJECTION

REFLECTION to projection is the process of being willing to examine our life: who, what, when, why and how, as we look to the future.

Now and then let's pause in our pursuit of happiness and just be happy. We do this by stepping back and questioning everything about our career choices, about our attitudes and beliefs, about the ways we choose to live. Are they healthy choices for us? This reflective process is the first step in solving challenges or creating the future. Reflecting can help open up new possibilities in our life. People who spend time in reflection tend to be more engaged in their lives, more fulfilled, and happier. They live more consciously.

The Glass in Your Car as a Metaphor

THERE are four important pieces of glass in your car: the two side mirrors, the driver's mirror, and the windshield. The driver's mirror is meant for us to quickly glance at what's behind us, where we've been in the past. The side mirrors are bigger but come with the warning, "Objects in mirror are closer than they appear." These mirrors create an illusion but allow us to see laterally. They don't support forward viewing or living. The windshield is the biggest piece of glass in the car. It is clear, and in bad weather, it is the surface we clean first to be able to see where we will be driving. The windshield allows us to focus on what's in front of us, what direction we are going, at what speed, and when we are near our destination. All surfaces are important to use to avoid an unpleasant accident; however, the windshield is the glass we use the most.

Reflection to projection involves "regression to progression." In throwing a ball, we have to pull our arm to a backward position in order to create the momentum to propel the ball forward and allow it to soar. This pulling back is the same action required to use a slingshot, shoot a rubber band, or send the arrow to the target in archery.

We can look at reflecting as developing and using critical thinking. Critical thinking is not negative thinking; it means to analyze something using a clear, rational process. We have a tendency to fall into the habit of going along with someone else's perception of who we are, or should be, or what we should do, and in doing so letting someone else or society set the program for our life. What others set may not necessarily be our dream, our passion, our soul's desire, or our rainbow. The danger of letting someone else set our program is we become comfortable with, or conditioned to, what works. Once we think something works we go for consistency, even if is detrimental, or not our true rainbow, or we are capable of so much more.

Reflection doesn't apply only to the past but where we are right now, in this very moment. We can see our own image when we look in the mirror. This will only reveal us as we "look" in the present. To look into our own eyes is difficult to do; we will look elsewhere, to our imperfections, to what we are wearing, how our hair looks—anywhere but directly into our own eyes. To do so scares most of us to death.

Yet reflection is a tool we can use to move forward.

What we become and what people see may be different. Most people don't want to open their eyes and truly see. Without opening our eyes, in the darkness of our mind, we can make believe life is whatever we want it to be. But when we open our eyes, we face reality. Using critical thinking helps us evaluate the truth of who we are, what we believe, and what is important in that moment. Truth may change as we grow. We have to sift through the changing reflections of life to discover our own truth. This is a never-ending challenge. The important thing is not to get stuck along the path but to keep learning and growing.

CONSCIOUSNESS

CONSCIOUSNESS creates our reality. Increasing our awareness is a serious goal in life. When we were born, our canvas was blank. Who drew the picture of our life? Who created the outlines and shapes? Who filled in the lines with colors as we were growing up? Are the shapes and colors a truth for us today?

Our biggest responsibility in life is to maximize our greatest potential. Yet, one of our utmost tragedies is not living our own truth. Instead we are living the physical, mental, emotional or spiritual consequences of someone else's plan for us, and when we do that we usually aren't happy. We should never allow ourselves to be defined by someone else's opinion of us. As Shakespeare wrote, "This above all: to thine own self be true... Thou canst not then be false to any man." To be our authentic self in a world that is constantly trying to make us something else is a great accomplishment. Let's be our best self, not an imitation of someone else.

The act of looking back on my experiences taught me that life brings challenges which appeared to be life-threatening, because I didn't have a clue how to deal with them. Even though I hadn't walked through these challenges before, I learned they can be successfully completed when you have faith and persevere. There is no better faith than faith based on experience.

Spending time reflecting on who we truly are and our talents is important. Finding the passion to be true to ourselves and finding the courage to take action allows magic to happen.

LESSONS FROM A SERIOUS INFECTION

IN 2014, I had a journey of being so sick with a serious infection throughout my body that I was right on the edge of dying. At the time, it was a very dark period. It was a struggle to come back. Now I think, "How could it have been so dark if today it shines such a light in my life?" That experience created purpose and opportunity for the light to shine!

Standing in the present and reflecting on the painful experience, I can now see its significance. To reflect at this point in my maturity makes it safe and healthy, because time and distance takes some of the pain and sting away from the experience. Now that I understand its purpose, the experience is no longer associated with pain! I recognize how it was necessary for my growth as a human being. It is the tempering of the steel in the fire. In the moment when steel is at its hottest, flaming red, it can be shaped, and when it is cooled down, it is a new shape.

Being at the edge of death, you don't have the answer as to why you went one way and not the other. We can call it protection by our guardian angel or ancestral spirits, who watch over us and know the script of our life. Part of their responsibility as spiritual ancestors is to pluck us from moments that will interrupt our destiny. They keep reaching in and snatching us out of situations and we don't know who, why, or how.

There were other turning points in my life where moments seemed really dark. Then, in seeing the way they played out in my life journey, they actually weren't that dark at all. If I had been the scriptwriter, I would not have written those experiences in, because they didn't feel good, taste good, or smell good. The way I was feeling at the time of the infection, there was no guarantee I would live.

As I've gone on in life, there have been challenges that I perceived, if through rose-colored glasses, to be normal at the time, but as I look around I realize my perception was skewed. In the area of, say, sex abuse, we either really withdraw and pull away from sexual relations, building a fortress around us concerning intimacy and become isolated, or we go to the other extreme, becoming promiscuous and having dysfunctional relationships. Or, if we have given up smoking or drinking, we can then become intolerant and judgmental of those who do smoke or drink. Even if we are no longer active in the dysfunction, these types of behavior do not lead to healing. It is said we teach where we've been; we serve where we've been. If one decides to take that attitude of service, terrible experiences can turn out to be positive.

L.O.V.E.

L.O.V.E is an acronym: Live Openly, Value Everyone.

Love is simply a four-letter word until it becomes action, by giving it meaning and letting our hands carry out the duties of our thoughts and heart. Love is a noun or a verb—not an emotion. Positive living in love means to live our life based on potential and not on emotion—to learn to grow, love, forgive and heal. Living with an absence of love brings chaos, abuse, hate, dysfunction, illness and disease (dis-ease=stress). Which do we choose?

Loving is a state of being. It is a way of relating to the world that is forgiving, nurturing and supportive. Loving is the ability to lift others up. Love dissolves negativity by focusing on the goodness of life. The inability to love is at the root of most of our problems. Some mistake love, compassion, and forgiveness as being submissive when they are actually empowering strengths.

As in martial arts, a rigid position becomes a point of weakness—for that which does not bend will break. Coming from a place of love creates a neutral position; we are not strongly attached to the outcome of a situation so that getting our way is no longer important. The neutral position of love brings acceptance of people, places, and things and allows for forgiveness.

FORGIVING IS "FOR GIVING"

WE cannot have the ability to love without the ability to forgive. Forgiveness is a component of love, and the absence of love is un-forgiveness. In order to heal our emotions or a situation, we must start with the willingness to forgive. Forgiveness is a decision we make not to treat our pain by causing pain in another. Knowing our own and everyone else's weaknesses gives rise to forgiveness and then to compassion. We must forgive ourselves first for our part in any situation. One has to love him- or herself enough in order to forgive another person. Forgiveness sets us free, because in loving ourselves we acknowledge that we deserve to be happy.

People don't see us as "we" are; they see us as "they" are. Therefore, to live openly and value everyone, we need to objectively see who others really are so we can respect them. This requires living in non-judgment and using discernment about the behavior of others. Discernment means to only decide what's right for our own self, not judging the actions of others. LOVE means we will only look down on another person when we are helping that person up. Real love is knowing someone's weaknesses and not taking advantage of them—knowing their flaws and accepting who they are.

All our efforts are rewarded with either love or lessons. If the outcome of our endeavor feels right, the reward is love. When it doesn't feel so good, it is a lesson to be learned, sometimes over and over again until we get it right. Love and lessons form the goal posts in life. We win the game of life when we go through those goal posts.

Love requires intimacy – that is, in-to-me-you see. It is being our authentic self at all times and communicating with compassion and honesty. That's not always easy to do. We need to support, encourage, and empower others to be the best they can be. When we, as unique individuals, accept others as unique individuals, this equals respect which leads to us functioning as one—or in unison. The equation is: $1+1=1$. In this way, love is the answer.

LOVE IS NOT ABOUT SEX

LOVE is not about sex, power or control. Sex is a physical act. Hugging is a physical act. Laughing and smiling are physical expressions. When we laugh, our eyebrows go up and a smile comes. But that is not what love is. Love is not the smile. Sex can be an expression of love but love is not the physical act. Sex doesn't need to be a component of love. I can smile and not be happy, just as we can have sex and not be in love. We should not confuse a physical act with the feeling, emotion, intention or experience of what love or joy truly is.

The word love is a huge umbrella covering a multitude of ways to express caring and appreciation—to live openly and value everyone.

Sex is only one way to express it. There are a hundred other ways to exhibit our love for someone. Love is simply about appreciation, respect and caring.

Love is not about possession either. If someone says he loves you, yet he is manipulating you, tearing down your self-esteem, or controlling you physically through violence, that is not love. That is an unhealthy obsession.

Love is sometimes about letting go. Everyone who is in our life is meant to be part of our journey, but not all of them are meant to stay until the end.

If we have the courage to recognize our challenges as spiritual signposts carrying messages for us, then we can gratefully accept these gifts and transmute them into lessons of love. And love is a healing force. Just as every problem proposes its own solution, every pain always contains the exact amount of love inside to soothe its own sting. It takes courage to live in love this way, with this attitude.

SELF-LOVE

UNDER the umbrella of love is the concept of self-love. Life is not set up such that if others don't validate us or give us all we need, we crumble and fail. When we "depend" on other people for validation, worth, and approval, then they control our destiny.

I travel often. I have had years where I've traveled 50,000 miles. I have heard flight attendants give their instructions thousands of times. Every time, they say the exact same thing the exact same way, "Put your mask on first before you assist others." The message is very clear and very consistent. If one of our ultimate objectives in life is to love other people, places and things, we have to put our mask on first—we have to love ourselves first. It is hard to give or offer something we don't possess. Self-love is where it all starts.

Kindness to one's self and all that surrounds us—people, places and things—is a powerful force. When we truly love ourselves we are going to want to express that physically, mentally, emotionally and spiritually. When we love ourselves, we will want to be as healthy as possible on all levels; we want to do only that which will contribute to our ultimate well-being and health. If we know that to be physically healthy we need to move our body, then moving our body becomes a priority. Why? Because we love ourselves that much. This same criteria applies to us on a mental, emotional, and spiritual level; taking care of our needs becomes a priority. How much of our spiritual or emotional power are we going to give away to someone else to be careless with? If we say we love ourselves, then we are going to make sure that we enhance every component of our being.

When we fall in love with ourselves, we take care of our health! We take on the responsibility for our own happiness. We invest in our passions. We are proud of who we are. We believe in ourselves, because we are worth it.

SELF-LOVE VERSUS SELF-CENTEREDNESS

WHAT we've been taught as self-love is often confused with self-centeredness. Self-centeredness is thinking everything is not just about me—it is ONLY about me. With a self-centered attitude, the world revolves around me and my needs first, above all else, even to the detriment and demise of others.

Self-love, on the other hand, is healthy and means taking care of ourselves. It is breaking that stereotypical energy where we've been taught not to be selfish. Some think, "If I take care of myself because I love myself, then I am being selfish," giving them license not to care about themselves, and by extension, others. This is not the case. In order to care about others, in a way that we are free and willing to give—in a healthy, loving way, we have to love ourselves enough to take care of ourselves first. We have to give to ourselves, so we are able and free to give to others.

Self-love includes setting boundaries. Part of taking care of ourselves is not allowing others to hurt or destroy us. This means not allowing others to destroy our spirit, to destroy our joy, to make us weak. If we have self-love we do not allow these things. Can we love something so much like our children, our spouse, our parents, our job, our faith or beliefs, our car—anything other than God—more than we love ourselves? We can't love God more than ourselves, because it is one and the same. But if we love any person, place, or thing more than ourselves, we give them control over our existence. Once we do that, we have nothing to offer, because we have given ourselves away.

As they say in the airlines, "Put your mask on first." Be content and strong in self-love.

"SELF-TASTIC" – BE FANTASTIC WITH SELF

TODAY, be "self-tastic." We exist in 3D: who we think we are, who others say we are, and who we really are.

We cannot run fast enough, or far enough, to get away from ourselves; everywhere we go, there we are! So, if we don't like, trust or believe the person in the mirror, then it is up to us to change something. If we have to, are willing to, and have the courage to walk away from the old us to discover the new, better, or best us, we should do it. The one absolute constant is that we will be with ourselves every second of every day, from the start to the finish of our life. No one can give us everything we need. Anything we have, we can also not have. But anything that we are, we can't not be! What we are can't be separated from us. For example, in my life you can't separate me from music, dance, and fitness. That is the core of my being, and the core of whom I AM. Who we are is from a single Source—God, if you will—from which we cannot be separated. As our love becomes more unconditional and accepting of ourselves, it begins to be experienced as an inner joy. This is a joy of unconditional kindness and respect for all life, including our own, and this condition may be referred to as compassion.

CHOOSING HAPPINESS

The purpose of life is to be happy
- The Dalai Lama

HAPPINESS is the joy we feel striving toward our potential. Our quest in life is to find something meaningful that gives us both increased satisfaction but also a sense of purpose. What we are passionate about, what brings us joy, and what makes our heart sing are all the same.

The amount of satisfaction we receive from life depends largely on our own ingenuity, self-sufficiency and resourcefulness. It is not easy to find happiness in ourselves, but it is not possible to find it elsewhere. People who wait around for life to supply their satisfaction usually don't find happiness. In addition, there can be no happiness if the things we believe in are different from the things we do.

It is interesting to note that the "pursuit of happiness" is a condition listed in the Declaration of Independence as being one of three unalienable rights along with life and liberty. And that these rights are endowed by our Creator. Do you think back then our Founding Fathers were onto something that we have perhaps lost sight of in today's world?

Happiness is something we find every day. Letting ourselves be happy is something between a responsibility and an obligation where, every day we say we are compelled to find our happiness, knowing that it is available. We don't have to manufacture what's already there. We have to push our ego out of the way and uncover it. Perhaps a better way to express this is to choose happiness every day by saying, "Today I choose…," then do what makes us happy.

When I say this in school assemblies, some students will challenge me saying, "Every day?" "Well, maybe not every day, only every day you breathe" is my response. Literally, happiness is a choice. We are taught that our happiness is someone else's responsibility, or our unhappiness is someone else's fault, or we have to struggle for happiness. We don't have to fight for it; we simply have to choose it! And it is ours, because we have been given free will.

The question to start the day with is: What does happiness look like to me? Do I choose "happy"? How do I do that? We need to question what happiness looks like to us, so we can choose it.

I've spoken to disadvantaged youths in Brazil and other places and told them the same thing. Even if you're a kid who wakes up in an impoverished area with little hope, the principle doesn't change. You don't find happiness; you choose it.

I put things in perspective by saying, "Okay, you're the captain of your day. You get to choose. What is it you have to choose between? Let's count—even though you are in an area rife with poverty, even though you are not sure where breakfast is going to come from—let's start on one hand and count your blessings. In spite of your situation, I promise you will run out of fingers and toes before you run out of blessings to be grateful for.

"Yes, you live in a poverty-stricken section of the city, but you weren't burned out of it last night. Yes, you have a hardscrabble existence, but no drug person came in and robbed you or shot your family." So, you start counting your blessings and then think, "Okay, I get to choose to be grateful and have joy knowing that I still have a day ahead of me. Or I get to choose to let the suffering of my situation lead my day and ultimately my life." The opportunity to choose between suffering or happiness is still available. It's real. Once we are taught to look at what we do have rather than what we don't have, we can make the choice.

Perhaps a person was in an accident and is now paralyzed or severely injured. He can still look at what he does have or can do versus what he lacks or what he cannot do. Personally, I am determined to be cheerful and happy in whatever situation I may find myself. For I have learned that the greater part of our misery or unhappiness is determined not by our circumstance but by our attitude. Our attitude is going to dictate the joy, happiness or peace we experience. We don't have to look for situations to choose happiness, they exist in every moment. We just have to acknowledge opportunity, know we have the freewill to choose positive emotions, rather than negative ones of anger and fear, and then practice making the choice over and over. That's where the work begins. The more we practice, the better we become at choosing happiness. Though the process is simple, it may not be easy.

Things I am passionate about bring me joy and make my heart sing. At this point in my life, the answer to what brings me joy and happiness is really simple. It is one word and that is, "love." Finally, you arrive at the point in life where you can say, "Oh, now I see how that event turned into a lesson and has played out in my life." Understanding my role, being a success in that role, surrendering to who I truly am, not someone's view of who I am, allows me to fulfill my number one Pepperism. This phase of awareness and consciousness gives me goose bumps on a daily basis. How can I not smile every day? Throughout my life, my father has been my number one example of smiling every day. In spite of what's going on inwardly, he always presents a smile.

Teaching classes at Step 1, presenting at conventions, talking to people individually, I have vehicles to share my happiness. I have an obligation to share my talents, and the fact that there are avenues for me to do so makes me grateful. My heart is happy, and it is my choice.

My soul is happy, and it is my choice. What I do with my body makes me happy, and this is my choice.

PERFECTIONISM

WE are born to be happy—not perfect. Perfection is an illusion. Perfection is a perspective; it is not tangible. A lot of our dysfunction comes from our concepts of what perfection is. Perfect is a learned concept. For example, you may look in a magazine and see Hollywood's opinion of what perfect beauty is. A photo, advertisement or text may suggest, "This is the perfect body; this is the perfect face." We forget what it took to create that image: how the photo was airbrushed or photoshopped, the plastic surgery that was used, the strict dieting, the host of people employed to achieve a certain look.

Some "expert" may point out what perfect success is: what the perfect American life is, what the perfect family is, what the perfect behavior at a specific age or in a certain environment is. All this is an illusion. And it is a weapon to make us feel less than happy.

Perfectionism reminds me of a dog chasing his tail, an infinitely elusive goal. It doesn't matter how fast the dog runs, he will never catch its tail. To me, we will never catch up to what we think perfect is. We will use our energy chasing this idea of perfection until we are so exhausted, we convince ourselves that we are an internal or external mess. Then we get down on ourselves for not being perfect.

We ignore the understanding that we are already perfect in what we perceive is our imperfection. Perfect or perfection is a judgment based on an illusion. We can spend our whole life searching for something we already have if we let go of the notion of perfection.

A certain concept of perfectionism does have its value; without it, there would be no striving to improve or grow. In a leadership role, we often use perfectionism as a tool to keep progressing. We teach, "Don't stop reaching; don't stop growing." I understand the intent, but when there is too much emphasis on perfection it puts the thought into our hard drive, "I've failed again," if we don't reach it. It sends the message that we're never going to be enough, we didn't go far enough, et cetera. We can also go the other way saying, "I can't be perfect, so why try" and shut down. For all of us, and especially for performers, we are rarely pleased with how we perform. There is always something to improve. The key is to maximize our greatest potential—not to be perfect, but to always attempt to do, and be, our best.

I was recently consulting with a mother who was trying to figure out how to guide her young son to change his attitude of perfectionism. He has to be first in everything—school, grades, sports, other activities—or he has an emotional meltdown. Something within him —or something externally—has taught him that if he doesn't win, if he doesn't come in first, if he isn't number one, then he's a total failure and has no value. Somewhere in his consciousness he's bought into the concept of perfectionism. The torture he puts on himself is unhealthy. Perfectionism is very detrimental for him. In speaking with his mother, I recommended putting different information in his hard drive and re-channeling how he evaluates that moment when he isn't number one or experiences the feeling of not being perfect. I suggested she explain over and over each time he has a meltdown that if he can be honest with himself and say he did his personal best, then he has won.

Who said perfection was a prerequisite for life anyway? The message comes from many sources. We instill that message unconsciously into our young. Youngsters are deciding what perfection means from their experiences as they grow. They experience angst and suffering for not meeting the self-induced expectation of being perfect. They are trying to figure out what perfectionism really means as they go through life, not knowing perfection is really an illusion.

My daughter, in her early twenties, got a tattoo on the side of her hand that exposes this lie about perfectionism. Written in cursive is the word "Enough," which means what God has given me is enough. Who I AM is enough; what I have is enough. I was chosen by God to be the best me I can be—and that's enough. This is the gratitude of acceptance. It was a huge lesson to me that someone so early in life understood the illusion of perfectionism.

MEDIOCRITY AND EXCELLENCE

ENOUGH isn't to be confused with mediocrity: doing less than our best, doing less than what's possible within us, doing less that fulfilling our greatest potential in what we are called to do. Enough is to understand we don't have to measure ourselves against anyone else's or society's idea of perfectionism.

Mediocrity is not a place to settle in life. How does attitude and character play into our being a sound human being? How does this play into our being a more productive worker? How does it decrease our sick days? These are the kinds of subjects I address in corporate talks. Then I bring in the concepts of how fitness, diet, and attitude contribute to our being a more productive worker or being more successful in our personal life.

Excellence is never an accident. Excellence is always the result of our high intention, sincere effort, intelligent direction, skillful execution and the vision to see obstacles as opportunities. Every job is a self-portrait of the person who did it. I choose to autograph my work with excellence. I choose to live by the saying, "The only way out is all the way in." Once you have had a taste of excellence, you cannot go back to mediocrity.

CHAPTER 7

Life in Sacramento

MY last post in the Air Force was in Sacramento in 1978. The next two to three years were my gypsy phase. Gypsy is a term for dancers in the theatre. After leaving the Tops in Blue world tour, I studied in New York City with Patricia Wilde, Maurice Hines, Madam Darvach and Frank Hatchett. I studied at the School of American Ballet, American Dance Center, Broadway Dance Center and STEPS. Next came studies with Gus Giordano in Chicago. Then in Los Angeles, I studied with Roland Dupree, Jackie Sleight and Joe Tremaine.

As a gypsy, you set up camp in a city long enough to study dance—living in hotels and waiting tables, or doing other temporary jobs to support yourself, but not long enough to develop roots. You always looked to study and perform at the same time. As an entertainer, or dancer in my case, you look for opportunities to study your craft, while at the same time always looking for performance opportunities or other jobs in the theatre. In New York City, I mostly did commercials about Broadway shows, industrial films, or "Welcome to New York" kinds of projects. I did some instructing.

While I was studying in L.A., I was residing in Sacramento. Even though my agent was in New York, I decided I wanted to stay in California. All the work she found for me in L.A. was from her office in New York. Even though I was working most of the time in Southern California—modeling, consulting, acting and performing—I still received my mail in Sacramento.

Everyone we meet contributes to our life, regardless of whether they know it or not. For me, early in my life, meeting the civil rights icons and Dr. King, and meeting members of the jazz bands, impacted my life back then and they still do today. In my travels, I have met some well-known people. I worked with Arnold Schwarzenegger when he was chair of the Governor's Council on Physical Fitness and Sports, long before he became governor. I did some things with Jack LaLanne and Gregory Hines. I was fortunate to meet Roxie Roker from the TV show

"The Jeffersons." Roxie played Helen Willis, half of the first interracial couple shown on prime-time television. I recognized that these people were doing what they were born to do. I said to myself, "That's the way life is supposed to be lived," because I couldn't see these people ever doing anything but what they were doing. I can't imagine B.B. King not playing "Lucille" on his guitar or Gregory Hines not tapping. I can't imagine Jack LaLanne not being involved in health and exercise. Jack was the first to open a health club in the United States in 1936 and to have an exercise show on television.

Meeting these people was a part of my destiny. None of them took me under their wing and acted as a mentor; however, they were very significant in showing me how you live your destiny. It was blatantly clear to me that you don't have to go out searching for what to do: what you are will find you.

On the other hand, there are people you meet who you don't invite into your life or develop a deeper relationship with, because they don't impress you or impact your life. Some people you meet, and the impression of that meeting lasts for a lifetime. Others you meet for only a moment.

I can look at my life now and know these people had an impact because they were all about following their path and living their greatest potential – and so am I.

SACRAMENTO

AFTER living in different cities and overseas, I felt I could be comfortable with Sacramento. The energy of the city had the potential to make my dreams come true, so I settled here when I was in my late twenties.

I stayed in Sacramento because of its size, growth potential and the pace of the city. Despite it being the state capital, I found it to be slower-paced compared to other places I knew, like New York and Los Angeles. I don't know if it's the farms around Davis or the politicians that are keeping it conservative, but it's a fact that we don't have a hard-core, big-city intenseness. The other thing I like about Sacramento is its cultural diversity.

When I moved to Sacramento in 1978, at first I didn't even get an apartment. I stayed in a hotel for a couple months before I started to look for work opportunities, checking areas of town that I might like to live in, and getting a sense of the overall energy of Sacramento. Still, as an international performer, choreographer, and show director, a large part of my work was outside Sacramento. Once I began to establish a life here I could look again at my education. During my first few years in town, I earned an EMT license, but my heart was still in dance and fitness. I produced and toured with the show Las Vegas on Stage in Japan during my early days here. I worked in commercials, in Las Vegas, national and international touring shows, and with my own dance companies.

MAGIC DANCE COMPANY

I first met Keith Goings when he was 15. Keith was dancing and saw me performing at a dance contest in Sacramento at the Woodlake Inn. From there, we became friends and I started the Magic Dance Company. Magic was a professional dance team of four men who possessed a strong desire to bring happiness to our audiences through entertaining shows.

When we started the Magic Dance Company, the four of us rented a house together where we lived, ate and slept. We trained all the time. I took Keith and the two other young dancers around to classes at different dance studios in town to work with the best teachers. We were doing local shows and television in town. We were living and working out of a building called the Model Center on Arden Way. It was a warehouse with a modeling school. They had open rooms, and we'd rehearse there. We did a lot of contests. To Keith, it was all exciting and creative.

"Pepper was always talking about technique, and I just thought he was a disco dancer. But he was really a professional dancer!" recalls Keith.

Disco was dying out, and eventually we all went our separate ways. Keith went on to dance at Great America theme park in the Bay Area. We kept in touch. He danced in Guam for several years, in Disneyland for seven years, followed by Disney World for about four years, before spending seven years in Las Vegas. He finally returned to Sacramento and Step 1 to teach.

Aside from Keith, some of my closest friends come from this time. I was teaching in several different locations. Touch of Jazz, a studio near Fulton Avenue and Alta-Arden, didn't have classes on Sunday. I was able to rent the studio for two hours on Sunday and had the place all to myself. I was teaching a class that was a combination of strength work, aerobics and stretch. Kim Goetz was one of my first students. After a while, she started collecting the money and signing people in for class.

Beginning in 1981, I taught dance at Sacramento City College for seven years as part of the adult education program. After Kim had been taking classes a couple of months with me at various locations, I suggested she take my dance class at City College.

"I looked at him and thought 'I don't dance,'" explains Kim. "But I went, mostly for the strength and stretch, because I'd never danced before. But once you get in class with Pepper, it's hard to leave. You can't just walk out, so you have to try. I was with him at City College for a couple of years before Step 1 opened."

I first met Mary Wright when she took a fitness class from me at an aerobic studio. She, too, began taking dance from me at City College. Next I started Bodytalks—a performing company with Kim and Mary as members. Alisa Shubb was involved in a local theatre production when Tyehimba, one of the dancers in Bodytalks, told her I needed a tap dancer and to come to my jazz class at City College. She came and eventually joined the company.

BODYTALKS

BODYTALKS Dance Company was a contemporary jazz and tap ensemble I put together. In the spring of 1985, Bodytalks presented "Dance Pages", a high-energy show featuring dynamic jazz, explosive tap, and expressive modern, performed in the City College auditorium. At the same time, I had been teaching English at local high schools for nearly five years. In a way, my English class was only my excuse to get teens into the classroom to teach them about life.

In the world of dance, the opportunity to be in a troupe often is based on looks and with whom you have trained. With the Bodytalks Dance Company, people were chosen to be in the company because they wanted to dance. It didn't matter to me what their shape was, what their look was. This was unusual for a performance company. We had the tallest, lankiest girl in there, and the shortest—it didn't matter. It didn't matter what their background or their training was. There was a girl in the company who had never had a dance class before, and she just picked it up and could make it happen. My goal in having the company was to give an opportunity to people who really wanted to dance, and who would work for it.

Alisa says, "Pepper is amazing. Whatever situation he finds himself in, he figures out the best way to handle that situation and to make that situation positive. With the Bodytalks Dance Company, he found how to make things work, to find venues for us to perform. He put a fitness team together, a dance team together; he found funding, and ways to go out and showcase what he does. He recognized early on how the fitness field would grow. He got into contests and traveled all around. At the same time, he was working really hard and making the best of every opportunity, which in turn lead to finding a business partner and opening a dance studio. Nothing's been given to him. He makes the most of every opportunity by looking out onto the horizon and asking what else is happening."

Because of my nature, I have to reach for the next step—what's beyond where I am now? Good enough was never good enough for me if there was a next level. That just followed a pattern I had set for myself early on. Even with everything else going on at this time, I continued with my education. After returning to college in the mid-80s, I graduated with a Master's degree.

Step 1 Dance and Fitness Studio Opens

YOU have to have a pioneering spirit in order to start your own business and build recognition in a new community. I carved out a niche for myself over seven years by teaching classes around Sacramento and at Sacramento City College. My day job was teaching high school. As my reputation increased, so did my class sizes, and I began to think about the next step.

Step 1 Sacramento Dance Academy opened in November of 1987 with Mary Wright as my business partner. Mary was always passionate about dance, and began taking my classes, following me wherever I was teaching. She had been dancing in Bodytalks for a couple of years when things changed in her life. She was working as administrator of a nursing home when a local hospital bought up all the nursing homes in Sacramento. The hospital didn't retain any of the management staff and Mary knew she didn't want to continue in that career field.

"I could tell Pepper had a big following, and it would be easier for him if his teaching was based in one place. Because of his draw and with my administrative background and our joint passion for dance, we thought, out of naiveté, 'Let's open a dance studio.' When we opened Step 1, we were very naïve," says Mary.

When Mary and I sat down to plan Step 1, we talked about what was going to be the nucleus of our belief by which we would operate and build the infrastructure of the business. We agreed it was relationships. We said, "We will never lose a relationship over a dollar." Thirty years later, we are practicing that same philosophy. I think that's something that carried over to me from my dad. If you lose people, you lose relationships, you lose faith, and you lose trust. When that happens, all your success doesn't matter.

The studio didn't happen overnight. It took us a while to find our location at 19th & T Street. We didn't have an existing business with a track record. At the time, people didn't even know what a fitness/dance studio was. Now it seems there's one on every corner. But back then, it was a rare business and hard to find a landlord who was willing to take a risk and build a 7,000 square-foot dance space. The wood floors were very expensive, and it was a hefty financial investment on the owner's part. It took us almost a year to find the location and a landlord willing to take a risk on us. Basically, the owners fronted a lot of money. They did take a huge deposit from us, which eventually we got back over the terms of our first couple of leases. We've been here 30 years now.

I'm the creative partner; Mary is the business partner. That's the way the business was designed, and that's why it's always worked for us. We respect each other's talents and that relationship lends itself to a balance.

"There's a relaxed flow between us. We never argue. We did at first, because Pepper's very grandiose in his ideas, and I'm not. I'm conservative, because I have the dollar to worry about. At first, we didn't have money to do things in the grand way he wanted to, which is the only way Pepper knows how to do things. He can't do things mediocre. I've come to accept that over the years. No matter what he does, it is always over the top, and that's just who he is—the perfectionist, the performer. Still, we work well together," relates Mary.

REEBOK FITNESS CHAMPIONSHIP

I'D seen the Reebok Fitness Championship competition and had some friends in fitness who were involved. Being competitive, it made sense to me to compete—the competition was about fitness, it was about dance, it was to music and it was performing on stage. I thought it would be fun and challenging. After all, it was all the things I was interested in, and it was taking my skill to the next level. I would have to work hard while striving to meet the contest standards. The possibility of progressing and moving forward to a national level was intriguing. I thought, "All this is great! I want to do this." I knew it would be a lot of work, and I've never been afraid of hard work. All the things most people considered hard work, I did for fun.

The Reebok Championship Team was made up of a mixed pair team (a male and female), a male solo, a female solo, and a trio team. I decided I was going to enter the competition as a solo. Then I thought a trio of three guys would be interesting, too. Even though a trio team had been done before, I had a completely different concept and vision. The dancers I had in mind for the team were both teaching at Step 1. Bernard Horn was teaching Hip-Hop and Jazz Funk and also dancing in the Step 1 Jam dance company. Keith Goings was working with the Metro Dance Company and teaching at Step 1 too.

I remember saying to them, "This is what we are going to do…" They looked at me like I was a Martian. They were dancers. They weren't into fitness. There is a fitness look versus a dance look versus a competitive muscle look versus a competitive dance look. It restricts your movements if you have too much muscle in dance—you need real strength and flexibility more. I would change my body depending if I was on a dance contract or a fitness contract. If you look closely, the subtle differences can be seen in my professional shots of the time.

During this period, I was also a member of the International Sports Medicine Association.

I said to Keith and Bernard, "Let's blend dance with fitness. That has never been done." The three of us were already doing shows together with dance numbers, so our flow and timing as a team was already present. We knew each other's moves. Without any question at all they both said, "yes," even though they didn't know what their commitment would entail. We trained for only two months before we competed.

Because we already had the foundation of a team, it didn't take us long to develop our routine. I had the schedule all set out. At 5:30 a.m., we met at the studio and worked out until 7:30. Mary was our only coach. She was there at 6:00 in the morning to watch us, make suggestions, and make us do it again. At 7:30, we'd go to our day jobs. We'd meet back at 3:30p.m. and train some more. We'd teach our classes at Step 1 and then have our rehearsals, staying until 11:30 or midnight. Then we'd be back the next morning at 5:30 to do the same thing all over again. We trained this way and worked on choreography at the same time. I'd bring in pots of spaghetti. We were eating and training, eating and training. That's all we did. I built my body bigger and bigger. No matter how tired or sore we were, when the three of us got together, the energy was electric—we were dynamic!

At the Pacific Regional Reebok Competition, I placed first in the Men's Individual category. Keith, Bernard and I placed first in the Team of Three category. I then had to choose which category I was going to compete in at the national competition. I chose the team competition, because I had two other people depending on my decision, and I knew they had put in as much work as I had. It wasn't about my individual success or validation, but ours as a team.

Winning Reebok's National Aerobic Championship earned us a contract with Reebok. As part of the Reebok Championship Team, we performed around the country and internationally. Mary and I thought winning the Reebok competition would be good for Step 1—it would be good advertising and get our name out there—but that's not what happened.

Bernard's, Keith's, and my energies contributed to the success of Step 1. Whenever we weren't there the energy was no longer the same.

"Pepper winning the Reebok National Aerobic Championship and being on tour for those two years almost put us out of business. When Pepper and the two other most popular teachers were traveling and not teaching consistently, attendance dropped," said Mary.

My Tops in Blue training was beneficial. Being responsible for managing people, the hustling to set up the show, performing, breaking things down, then getting the troupe to the airport and finally on the tour bus to the next show came in handy. The tour bus would take the Tops in Blue team to the theatre, we'd do the show, then it was the reverse: back to the tour bus to the airport to the next location. If it wasn't across the country, then you got on the tour bus to the next city, repeating this cycle every day. We got two days off a month! Tops in Blue went to the Far East and to Europe. All this prepared me for the rigorous schedule of the Reebok tour. The schedule and duties for Reebok were much the same. We had to set up the stage and per-form—we were the show!—then break everything down and move on for the next city and show.

Keith Goings still teaches at Step 1 every Sunday and, after Reebok, went on to Solid Gold and a successful dance career. Bernard Horn moved to Texas and, to my knowledge, stopped dancing and has a graphic design business. He's a family man. For me, a contract with ESPN came on the tail end of the Reebok contract. I was under con-tract with ESPN a little over three years. I was seen on cable TV's ESPN network as a principal co-host of the program "ESPN Fitness Pros." We filmed on location—like St. George, Utah at the Green Valley Health Spa, a resort with beautiful red mountains in the background as our stage.

MY ARTISTIC LIFE

I'M sure, not unlike most people, my entire life has been about sur-vival. One of my chief gifts to help me survive is artistry—music and dance. I am grateful to be able to use that still today to express myself and to be able to put it on stage. My life could have gone in a totally self-destructive way if I didn't have music and dance, if I didn't have something to turn to when I was younger, and didn't understand why things happened to me.

Throughout my life, my creative talents have given me hope. Life is difficult when it is not so obvious what your talents are. For those who do not have the same level of passion and ability it could be easy to feel like they are nothing or have nothing to contribute. Some of my siblings did turn to self-destructive ways. They were not as musically inclined, and they weren't into art, dance and movement. Their lives went in a totally different direction.

Showing up at auditions and facing rejection, getting into a show, working to discover what the show means, discovering the process of developing working relationships, understanding the struggle you go through to effectively deliver the message, learning how versatile you have to be, and how talented you have to be to meet demands— these are all forced opportunities for growth. Some may say, "Oh, that person is talented," but if you are talented, your responsibility to that talent is greater. To those whom much is given, much is demanded, or it is a case of not hiding your light under a bushel. Yet, we still have free will whether or not to discover and honor that talent.

For me, if it's creative and artistic, if there's movement to music creating a picture, I've always been excited about the project. I don't care if it's a benefit for the community, for students, for schools, for live theatre or for television. I have a diverse performing background, with dance and fitness being my passion.

The only way this life works for me is living through my heart. I think that's the answer to many of our problems as a society. I'm on a mission to unify people's hearts and to impact the lives of all ages in a positive way. Dance is my calling; it's not just what I do but who I am—how I touch the lives of others. For me, dance and fitness are the vehicles for my purpose in this life.

I began my dance training as a child, starting with tap, then bal-let, which I found too restrictive for my "hyper personality." Yet, as an instructor, I stress the importance of ballet training to students every chance I have. Jazz followed, for which I found myself perfectly suited.

While my choreography can at times be filled with story and symbolism, I see my role as one of pure entertainment. The numbers I choreograph are just like a number you'd see on Broadway—there's flash, flare, glamour and high energy.

I strive for performances that are always upbeat and positive. The message may not have had a happy ending, but it always delivers a positive message. When I wrote and produced "Let's Go," the show touched on really deep subjects, but it is positive and upbeat. There can be darkness, but what I want to give the audience is something that is uplifting and demonstrates rising above challenges. Hopefully, those watching also find humor that brings a smile. I try to make things fun.

"LET'S GO!"

IN 2008, I created my own show from scratch called "Let's Go!" which received an Elly Award for Best Choreography of a musical production. The show highlights 22 talented singers and dancers at odds to determine which group will reign supreme. Throughout the production, the opposing entities compete for the spotlight, first as rivals and then as a team. "Let's Go!" takes you on a roller coaster ride of emotions through its inspirational stories of loss, hope, rivalry, connection, fear and love. Throughout the first act, the singers and dancers battle each other to see who's the best. But the magic begins when the rivals realize the only way to be number one is to act like number one. United through a tragic loss, the performers come together in act two to find out it's possible to overcome obstacles and live their dreams and put on a show.

Through information, inspiration, and motivation, "Let's Go!" creates the atmosphere, sets the stage, and offers the tools for real improvement in morale and conduct. These tools improve the ability to combat such insidious enemies as self-destructive and antisocial behaviors in performers and audience members alike.

The music includes Broadway tunes, R&B, country, rock, gospel, salsa and hip-hop. Dynamic dance numbers in jazz, tap, African, hip-hop, contemporary and Latin styles are performed. "Let's Go!" has had three phases or versions so far. The first phase was written as being all musical. The second phase became scripted, and the third phase has more content and characters in the script.

There is an old saying that, in order to be successful, we have to write about what we know, then it is authentic. Parts of "Let's Go!" are autobiographical. Those parts are hidden, but I know they are there. The cast does moments of singing and dancing with great energy, and it is very powerful, but they don't know if it's fiction or nonfiction.

I never sat the cast down and identified which were components of my real-life experience.

The homeless lady dying, the absent father, siblings that didn't know each other existed but come together through their life journey and find out they are siblings, the son angry with his father for taking off and leaving the mother to raise him, and carrying that anger through to dysfunctional personal and social behaviors, the angry son who had a daughter—all these elements are found in the musical.

"Let's Go!" means a lot to me for many reasons. It signified components of my reality, but it also gives me another huge vehicle to share and impact other people's lives.

"HUMANITY 6"

THERE is a part of the "Let's Go!" process where six cast members come out on stage and do miniature interviews.

From the audience's point of view, the performers all look like happy, shiny faced, energized people living their dream, clapping and singing and dancing. Then the curtain is closed, the lights are out, the applause has stopped, and now you've got real people.

After the curtain, singers and dancers sit on the stage to talk directly to the audience. What they share with the audience is unscripted. There is no preconceived dialogue, no rehearsal, no makeup, no costumes. They reveal their innermost life stories—components of their pain or themselves. They share how music and the camaraderie of bringing a show to the stage changed their lives.

The audience discovers those performers are real people like themselves. The performers tell, in their own words, how they made it over the humps in their lives. And members of the audience can relate and say, "That is me. That was me over and over and over again."

Therapeutically, this goes both ways. It could be totally crushing for the actors, or it can be healing for them as well as healing for people in the audience. The whole idea behind "Humanity 6" was for each cast member to have the opportunity to say, "This event in my life almost took me out. I am so grateful there was dance, singing or art. Because what you saw tonight was the actor playing a part, but now you see me as a real person."

The cast members step out of their character and share their own stories. The unspoken message is, "I know there is someone out there right now in the audience that is in the same pain I was when I didn't know how I was going to make it." This sharing lets them know there is something he or she can attach to that's healthy, and that he or she will be okay, too. The performers say, "I found something that got me to the next level, and you can do the same thing."

The moral of the story is: "I found help. The doors were open, but I had to put forth the effort and work damn hard to take advantage of that opened door. Sometimes I worked day and night. There is a lot of work that comes with being well."

"Humanity 6" serves to acknowledge and discourage self-destructive, unhealthy behaviors through reflection on one's dreams, goals, and choices. The cast illustrates this through their testimony, their personal journeys to healthier, more successful lives. Following the template of "reflection to projection," they are able to bring their life paths back into their natural, proper focus. They found the power to say "no" to the temptations and "yes" to the hard work and tremendous gratification of life. They share their realizations.

I was invited, and took, "Humanity 6" to the Air Force several times in the Sacramento area. My contact in the Air Force was a morale officer who set the performances up with the base general.

"A CHORUS LINE"

IN July 2008, I choreographed "A Chorus Line" for director Brent Null. The musical follows dancers trying out for a Broadway production while offering a metaphor for life's successes and disappointments. I really identify with the role of Mike, the tap dancer who had to attend dance lessons with his sister and who sings "I Can Do That."

The cast were not dancers who had trained since they were ten. They were people who had lessons here and there, but they all wanted to perform. I told them going in, "If you let me, I will grow you through this experience. If you'll get out of your own way, you will not leave this show the same person as when you came in. And if you take that growth and give it to the audience, they will leave the theatre changed from when they came in. That's what this show is about.

I know what it is like to pay and pay and pay, and work and work and struggle to get on the stage. I identify with those people who are not giving up on their passions. You cannot appear on the stage cloaked in a cocoon, safe and guarded. You've got to be willing to be vulnerable."

Writing productions like "Let's Go!" with its theme song "Dare to Care" and choreographing shows such as "A Chorus Line" are just part of my calling. I have so much passionate commitment to local theatre. There is a fine performing arts community in the Sacramento area, and any small part I can play in bringing that out, in making it better, I want to contribute. I want to challenge the complacency of community theatre here. I want to go to the edge, wherever that is.

"Smokey Joe's Café"

"Smokey Joe's Cafe" is a dazzling song and dance celebration of 39 of the greatest rock and roll songs ever recorded and written by the team of Jerry Leiber and Mike Stoller. It is an expression of American culture through outstanding entertainment. Beginning in 1995, "Smokey Joe's Cafe" ran on Broadway for four years, making it the longest running musical revue in Broadway history. I was cast in the local production and won an Elly Award for Best Supporting Actor in a Musical.

Garbeau's Dinner Theatre

I choreographed "Sing! Sing! Sing!" which was perhaps the most emotional sequence ever staged in Garbeau's history. In this commemoration of WWII, civilians finish singing a gospel song as sirens begin to wail while an intense battle scene is staged through modern dance. The battle ends. Soldiers either survive or fall, and a mother receives "The Letter" that her son will not be returning home. A lone soldier, struggling under the weight of the American flag, calls for help to raise it, forming the famous image on Iwo Jima. Countless troops, veterans, and civilians proclaim that this is a truly poignant and inspiring depiction of "America the Beautiful."

I also was a choreographer/dancer at Garbeau's Dinner Theatre in "Cabaret" and "Chicago." For the Sacramento Ballet, I've been a dancer in the "Nutcracker" and "West Side Story." For the San Joaquin Ballet, I performed in "Giselle."

ON STAGE AS A PERFORMER

"As a performer, Pepper is a bundle of fire—an energy ball," says Keith Goings. "When he's performing, there is an excitement from him about being there. Some people are so deadpan when they perform, but Pepper lights up on stage. You can be as technical as you want, but you have to have some style, some personality that comes through. He's magic—that's where our name Magic Dance came from. Magic was the four of us."

Long-time student, Jackie Anderson, says, "As a performer, Pepper is dynamic. He brings you in and creates magic. He can perform anything. Not just dance and fitness things, but just talking with him is inspiring. Like everything else, Pepper throws himself all into a part—there's no halfway about anything that Pepper's involved in."

To business partner Mary Wright, Pepper is always a performer. "He teaches classes as a performer. Every time he steps in front of people, it's a performance. He brings the magic with him. It doesn't matter what the class is; when he's in front of people, he's always in that performance mode—always. That's a constant."

"Pepper shines as a performer," notes Janice Mitchell. "He is dynamic. He's a brilliant dancer and choreographer. His magnetism turns on; he lights up. He has a sparkle in his eye. Pepper is like that a lot in everyday life. He can be very witty and funny and quick. He has a presence about him that, on stage, is electrifying."

WE ARE ALL CHOSEN

I was chosen by God to be who I am, and given the gifts I have to fulfill my greatest potential – to be the person I am and do what I do. Yes, I have been given many talents, but so have you! We are all chosen. Our mission is to embrace who we are through self-love. To deny who we are is not worthy of us.

There is something that only each of us can do better than anyone else. We need to listen to our inner voice and bravely obey it. Thinking critically and listening to our instincts will tell us what to do, but it's our personal power that will actually create the deed. We can start small by nurturing ourselves, by giving ourselves permission, time and room to grow—by loving ourselves and forgiving ourselves. In a year or two, we will blossom. We, and only we, have the power to change our life.

Each of us has magnificence (defined as: greatness or splendor, richness of appearance, or great beauty), because we are magnificent (defined as: wonderful, splendid, glorious, brilliant, outstanding). Let's be open to our magnificence, and let life bring us magnificent joy and inspiration.

Those who have nurtured us, taught us, invested in us, loved us, and empowered us to maximize our greatest potential have given us two things: roots and wings.

Live it,
Breathe it,
Be it,
Then give it away.
Go Be You,
Achieve your greatest potential!

Make the world a better place for you having lived in it.

CHAPTER 8

Building Community

WHEN things go wrong, many of us look outside ourselves for a cause. Some adults learn to get past this tendency, however, and are open to accepting responsibility. Emotionally immature people just go with their blame instinct and create drama. I don't choose drama. Sometimes we may not step aside quickly enough, but given a choice, I don't get caught up in emotional drama. I don't waste my time in the energy of someone's drama.

I feel one of our greatest challenges in life is taking responsibility for our own dreams, choices, families and communities, and maintaining self-respect as well as respect for others. Focusing more on keeping God first in our lives and teaching our youngsters by example are additional challenges we face.

EMOTIONAL INTELLIGENCE

EMOTIONAL intelligence, as a psychological theory, was initially developed by Peter Salovey and John Mayer. It was introduced and brought to the attention of the public by David Goleman in 1995. Goleman's book, Emotional Intelligence, proposes a counterargument to the theory that Intelligence Quotient (IQ)—the common measure of assessing a person's intelligence—is genetically given and cannot be changed by life experience. Goleman asserts that Emotional Intelligence (EI) is more important than IQ. EI, which includes self-control, persistence, enjoyment in life, and the ability to motivate oneself, is a skill which can grow through life experience and can assist us in reaching our full potential as individuals.

Briefly, our level of EI is defined by how effectively we perceive and relate to our emotions. There are four main components at play: 1)emotional awareness, 2)regulating our emotions, 3)harnessing those emotions and 4)being highly perceptive, or sensitive to the feelings of others.

I certainly subscribe to these thoughts. However, a spiritual approach can also be taken that adds to our understanding of ourselves. For instance, a baby is not "new." Everyone already comes into this life with a certain amount of information, knowledge, innate talents, or maturity. Just like we have to go through schools before we can graduate, this happens to be "earth school." There are certain experiences we have to learn in earth school in order to discover who we really are and what our talents are. When we find ourselves in certain situations, we can either blame ("be-lame") others or step back, see the big picture, and make a strong decision to take the most effective action.

Whatever decisions we make, or actions we take, do so as an adult. Do so with forethought. Do so understanding that no one can do these things for us, so we need to do them well. If we tend to hold ourselves accountable, we'll welcome others to assist us. We'll see others as allies when they don't let us off the hook. In fact, our best friends are those who won't settle for excuses. Our most powerful weapon against self-sabotage is our own honest self-awareness. Everything we do to expand our self awareness contributes to our maturity as a person.

Sometimes a person with this kind of maturity is referred to as an "old soul." That description encapsulates a lot of otherwise unexplained awareness or knowledge. I've always been referred to as an "old soul." As we grow into our own beliefs, we can better understand who we are.

My approach to life goes back to the lesson I learned from my grandmother, when she told me to leave a place better for my having been there than it was before I got there. If I can share that one concept, and people of all ages grasp it and apply it, I'm happy. I've learned that everything in life is transitory and building to something else. That gives us hope. Our job in life is to get through whatever the current challenge is we face and trust the process, even though it may be 20 years down the road before we can understand what that experience was about and why it was necessary.

We can't give people what they already have; however, we help give them access to the tools they need if they believe the tools are accessible. The tools are there—maybe they aren't yet sharpened, and people need to learn how to use them—but the tools are there.

"Pepper gives and gives to the community, to those in need—he gives his time, talent and heart. For instance, he worked with delinquents in a youth detention facility. These were really troubled kids, and he'd go in there and try to show them another way. I watch him in the studio with all the little dancers, and some of those kids are pretty underprivileged. He's always kind to them. He bends down and gives them hugs and gives them love. It reminds me of the saying, 'A man is tallest when he bends to help a child.' Pepper gives so much, not only in the studio but out in the community as well. He leads with his heart," shares Jackie Anderson, who has known Pepper many years as a long-time student at Step 1.

WORKING WITH THE SCHOOLS

ONE of my passions is working with troubled youth. I'm involved with an organization of community-based mentors and life coaches in programs for youths who are confused, angry and uncertain. We help students find motivation and direction in their lives. We have worked in juvenile detention lockdown facilities and in truancy counseling. We're there to show the students their potential. Youths come in and they're so hard, so uninterested—that's the way they survive. We engage them. We say, "Let me help you."

With my strong passion to spread the importance of education to our youth, I realized the school system wasn't as progressive as it could be. Therefore, I joined a community group, contributing my talents and skills, and we came up with a way to help this youth population. For my part, I use dance and discussion to emphasize the importance of education and to motivate young people to treat themselves and others with respect. At school assemblies I speak about drugs, teenage pregnancy, gangs, guns and violence. I wrote and recorded "The Gun," an original song to encourage the decrease of gun violence.

"ENOUGH IS ENOUGH"

THE California State Constitution affirms that students and staff have the right to attend safe schools. Our anti-bullying project for school-aged children is called "Enough is Enough." "Enough is Enough" is an innovative prevention program, with an evidence-based, research-supported approach. Our group's intention is to help decrease student absenteeism and increase student achievement. We believe that effective schools are safe schools. The program is designed to assist schools and communities in recognizing, understanding, defining, and responding to abusive, antisocial behavior. Our mission is to help decrease threats to safety in our neighborhoods for students going to and from school, as well as on campus. Through raising awareness, increasing education, and encouraging intervention and prevention by providing resources, support, and interactive programming, this program assists students in regaining self-esteem, self-worth and self-respect by reclaiming their personal power.

I was a Youth Program Instructor for the Health Education Council as well as an educator for the Elk Grove Unified School District's Nutrition Olympics. At all these gatherings, I communicate with students on their level—using street language and wearing "cool" clothes. By sharing my own stories, I encourage students to open up.

We present at assemblies to all grade levels throughout Northern California. We introduce fitness and the importance of health by teaching funky dance steps and providing practical health information. The sessions end with a message of encouragement. I emphasize respecting yourself physically, as well as mentally. My goal is to empower students to turn away from gangs, gun violence, and drug abuse, directing their focus to positive goals in order to make a long, healthy and happy life for themselves.

Community advocate, Greg King, talks about his work with Pepper at school assemblies: "Dressed in baggy, faded jeans rolled once above his name-brand athletic shoes, an oversized denim shirt partially unbuttoned to reveal a large, silver cross around his neck and a blue bandana covering his head, he fits in with the kids when he was actually the age of some of their parents. He's cool and very effective at getting his message across."

The mission of the "Enough is Enough" program is to provide students with resources, educational tools and experiences that will help them adjust in a positive way in their schools, their families, and their communities. Participation in antisocial daily activities and overall lack of achievement leads students into conflict and instability. Lack of social support makes it more likely for students to display negative behavior. Through community interaction and life planning, we focus our efforts on addressing dynamic and changeable factors, and on building multi-level relationships in schools. We do this by standing together and declaring that: "Enough is Enough." You will no longer allow bullies to steal your joy or control your lives. "Enough is Enough" inspires a positive change in students by having them reflect on their choices and introducing them to pro-social activities and programming. In the process of projecting their dreams, students will show change and become catalysts in their families, their schools and their communities.

For years, I went to elementary and high schools in troubled areas to talk with kids about the importance of education and saying "no" to drugs. We'd go to elementary, middle and high schools where we'd aggressively reach out to the large number of black children who are often surrounded by drugs and violence. We worked to instill a sense of hope.

We'd do lectures, aerobic demonstrations, and aerobic dance and fitness classes in an assembly form. We'd talk about keeping their lives and hearts together. We'd tell them to stay in school, to stay away from drugs, to have goals in life. The students talk and listen. I try to be as tangible as possible, and I have accepted the challenge of helping them feel that somebody is encouraging them to be the best they can be. It's their choice—adults may put on the pressure, but it's the kids' choice to make it in life. I love doing this. Someone has to take a chance on our youth.

Over the years, the teachers who have requested I speak to students find that my discussion on fitness, nutrition, mental attitude and general health supports and enhances the students' science curriculum. My abundance of knowledge, combined with humor and a "general ease of being," keeps students engaged and responsive. They also have an opportunity to share what they know and practice what they've learned. Health, good nutrition and exercise are lifetime goals.

Some of the teachers, who work with students who have failed several classes and are in danger of dropping out rather than successfully continuing their education, also gain invaluable skills and tools to help motivate students to stay in school and succeed. As Terry Ross, teaching at-risk kids in a 1992 summer school program, writes, "Although I received excellent educational training at Stanford University where I received my Master's degree and teaching credential, and despite teaching English in several types of high school environments, nothing could have prepared me for the enormity of difficulties facing these students." Ross invited me to speak to his students and others in the summer high school program. I spoke for approximately an hour and a half about self-determination and motivation. I spoke to the students in a language they could understand. Later, if students had difficulty concentrating or producing work, Ross would remind them of my speech and their own ideas they had written in their journals about my presentation. Ross credits my visit as being a turning point for the students.

"DREAM COLLECTIVES"

ANOTHER program I co-founded called "Dream Collectives" is a youth-based, life skill-enhancement program focusing on choices, self-esteem building, education, test-taking strategies, nutrition, health and fitness, drug and gang awareness, and intervention and prevention. "Dream Collectives" was on campus three days a week, two hours per day, providing prevention and intervention services, case management, and home visits through street outreach services. At the end of each three-month period, a stage production performance gave the students in the program an opportunity to recognize their talents in the areas of visual and performing arts. This gave the students an opportunity to work collaboratively and effectively with their peers in the process of fulfilling their creative dreams. We also helped develop a peer-to-peer conflict management team.

SSTARR POWER

SSTARR is an acronym for: Stimulant, Stop, Think, Assess, Respond and Recover. SSTARR is a system for conflict management. The system came into being when I was working with delinquents in a youth detention facility (YDF), because so many of them went from Stimulant, skipping over Stop, skipping over Think, skipping over Assess, and going straight to Response. And their actions had life-altering consequences.

In hindsight, the residents are asked to reflect on the action that got them where they are by thinking about the following:

S=Stimulant:
What sets you off; what makes you angry; what gets you riled up?
S=Stop, Look and Listen:
Pause in the moment before you do anything.
T=Think:
What am I about to do; what will the cost of that action be?
A=Assess:
Weigh the thing that is about to happen against the ramification of your action.
R=Respond:
Finally, action! What are you going to do?
R=Recover:
Healing from the event or consequences of the action taken.

I know how going from Stimulant (what sets you off) to Response (the action or reaction, skipping over the other steps) happens. If you'd asked me to do SSTARR before the moment when my father stopped me from killing another teen whom I was told had raped my girlfriend, I would not have been capable of doing these steps. Fortunately, my father was there to act as the STOP. He knew he had to stop me from making a huge mistake in my life. This experience allows me to understand what these young offenders have gone through. I have no judgment about them being in detention. I know what it's like to be in the situation they were in—the very moment that changed their life forever and landed them in the detention facility.

The groups I dealt with in the YDF were street-smart, sophisticated kids. They were hard-core. They had taken a life, and they were only 13! When I looked at them, my heart went out to them. Of course, they are reacting out of a learned behavior, ricocheting and reflecting off their environment. They, too, were victims in a sense.

Initially, some of the offenders were sent to the SSTARR class by the court, by their caseworker, or by their probation officer. It was written in their daily activity that they had to attend. When they could see progress in how they felt about themselves and their actions, light bulbs would go off. They would start being creative, writing poems, and being more reflective and less agitated.

The SSTARR session was not part of their school time. When the class became voluntary—this was one of the things they could do in their "free" time as an optional activity—instead of playing sports, they kept coming. That's when I knew it was having an effect. Their willingness to be proactive was important. To see possibilities after so much damage and pain, to witness certain youth come out of the program and become counselors was rewarding. Some became junior ambassadors in their own neighborhoods after leaving a gang.

The A in SSTARR stands for Assessment. Assessment involves thinking about the benefit and the risk of the possible action. This involves weighing the balance of whatever happened against the ramification of their reaction: is the potential action in balance with the stimulant? For example, they are asked: "What set you off? Was it some punk in the neighborhood coming up to you when you were wearing new Nikes and intentionally stepping on your foot, scuffing them up, maybe even beyond repair? Does your shooting or knifing him balance his aggression? Is it worth spending your life in jail for instant ego satisfaction, because he ruined your new shoes?"

The final freedom coming before actions is free will or choice. Once we are able to acknowledge the choice we made in a more compassionate state, after realizing the impact of our choice and the consequences to ourselves and others, we progress toward remorse. We regret what happened and can consciously decide not to act in the same way next time based on the now known consequences.

However, with that being said, there are things we can never undo. It is like posting something hurtful on social media. Even though we regret later having posted it, thinking that was a horrible idea, we can't pull it back. Whatever we said is out there on the Internet and, even if we wanted to, we can't take back what we wrote. It is too late. Our post is going to affect someone in a negative way or perhaps hurt many people—some we may not even know.

Those in the youth detention facility had committed an act that was violent. In their case, the SSTARR process was too late, but they could put it to use in the environment in which they now found themselves. They, and we, can find our passion where our anger is. But in their case the method of expression of their passion was a toxic anger.

People usually get angry or upset about things they have a really deep-seated passion about. The challenge is to transform anger into positive energy that through creativity expresses joy and lifts spirits.

Students could understand the analogy of the "Nail in the Fence" I often shared with them. It is a message of remorse and regret they can understand without feeling "preached to."

THE NAIL IN THE FENCE

AS you are walking past, you notice someone has just built a wonderful new fence. They have put a lot of effort into making it perfect. The workmanship is of excellent quality. All the boards are made to match and are the same height; it has flawlessly been painted a beautiful color.

Because of the day you are having, to make yourself feel better you have an urge to damage the fence by taking a hammer and pounding a nail in it. Once you've done that, now every time you pass that fence and see that nail, it reminds you of how you felt that day, how angry you were. The pain was so great you wanted to damage something, so you did.

Then one day you realize you damaged someone's property. You've scarred the beautiful fence forever. And you think, "I didn't really mean to do that. I really did it to make myself feel better. I didn't mean any real deep harm." So, you decide you are going to take back your action. You go get a hammer and pull the nail out. "Ah, better!" you say to yourself.

But the problem is the fence still isn't like it was. Now there's a hole. "You say to yourself, "Crap, that didn't make the fence look much better." So, you go get some wood putty and patch the hole. You sand it and paint over it. No one will be able to tell there had been a hole. But you will know.

As children, how many times do we try to fix things so are parents will never know? In our mind that works, but in reality it never really does. Our parents are wise to us.

You patch up the hole, sand it smooth, paint over it, and anyone casually passing by wouldn't see the hole. Yet, anyone who pays close attention and focuses on details, especially the fence itself, can see that one board is not like all the others. No matter how sorry you are, you can't make it perfect again. You can patch up the hole but not fix it.

Another example of "patching" is when you fall and break your arm. The bone will heal, except an X-ray that goes deeper than the surface of the skin will show the break by more calcification where the bone healed. It is the same thing—the body heals, but a history of injury always remains.

As a consequence of their actions, youths who shot people or have taken a life, even in their deepest remorse when they are truly sorry, are now paying with their own life. The scar that it leaves on them and a family is forever. It can be forgiven, but it can't be undone.

One day, a package came addressed to me. It was a book a fourth grade teacher was reading to her students—a story about an empty chair. In the story, a boy and his brother run into gang members on their way to school. They get into a fight, and one boy is killed. The story is about how the killing affects his family, the other students in his class who don't have him sitting in his chair anymore, and how that incident affected the shooter's family. I read the book to the youth. I shared with them about my own childhood growing up.

My files are filled with thank-you notes and letters from teachers and students at different schools and many grades. Teachers would often have their students write me thank-you notes with pictures they drew. I sometimes would chuckle when I read them. One student wrote in his thank-you note that what he learned from the book was not to walk to school! Hmm...

My early experiences in life prepared me to do this work. I share with students that there is a 100% chance they are not alone. What they're going through is probably all too common. That should settle the question of whether or not life is singling them out. The challenge for them is to learn how resourceful people deal with their particular challenge: to change their knee-jerk reactions, to think before they act, to not let their emotions override their intelligence, to deal with the facts instead. None of this is easy, but it can and does happen with effort.

The final R in SSTARR stands for Recover. The process is not complete until one recovers by learning and healing from the branding incident. There are tools to combat self-destructive and antisocial behaviors. Events cannot be undone. They can, however, be forgiven by all parties involved. Tools for healing and taking a proactive approach include forgiving themselves and others, using meditation for clarity, praying for strength and wisdom, and doing the work of digging deep within themselves to find the courage needed to take the steps to change behaviors.

SSTARR Power isn't just for troubled youths. There are many times in life when the lessons in SSTARR work; they may apply in many situations we find ourselves in. For example, I learned in scuba diving that emergency situations call for a logical response or things go bad quickly. Say we can't breathe, and suddenly we panic and shoot to the top. Our knee-jerk reaction has taken over. This knee-jerk reaction is not the best response in this scenario and can have disastrous results. The bends, also known as decompression sickness, occurs in divers when dissolved gases caused by bubbles of nitrogen gas form in the blood and tissues when the diver ascends too rapidly. The bends can be incredibly painful and a potentially deadly condition. In scuba training, we had to learn to manage our reflex actions to avoid the bends.

Retraining knee-jerk reactions applies in personal relationships as well. Following the steps in SSTARR allows us time to pause in the moment before we say or do something that we can't take back. It gives us time to ask, "What will be the cost of the action I am about to take? Is what I am about to do in line with what happened or am I being overly sensitive?" In answering these questions, we allow ourselves to look at things from the other person's perspective. Perhaps they didn't mean what we heard. Or their intention was not to hurt us; they just phrased things poorly. Our communications with others not only affect our own health mentally, physically, emotionally and spiritually, but the other person's as well. Practicing the steps in SSTARR gives us compassion in our relationships with others. It gives us the opportunity to apologize, allowing for forgiveness and healing.

As I've outlined, SSTARR is for everyone. I do something similar, but more sophisticated, with adults, linking it to conflict management and resolution. The acronym and steps are the same. The concepts, however, are more complicated in conflict management when applied to family dynamics or in the corporate setting.

However, in any challenge we can ask, "What can I do to help make the situation better?" Listening to the voice within will direct us. We will not get caught up in the problem and fail to engage in the solution. Nevertheless, if we find there is no answer, there is no problem—that is, there is no way to make the situation better. In this case it is best to leave the situation alone for the time being until a solution is forthcoming.

COMMUNICATION IS A KEY

TODAY we are practicing fewer and fewer tools of effective communication, tolerance, compassion, and forgiveness; we're less and less compassionate, less and less tolerant, less and less flexible. All these things that cohesively hold relationships together are now missing because we spend so much of our time with our electronic gadgets. As a result, our most precious commodity, our youth, falls through the cracks. It doesn't matter the economic strata of society in which you are—whether it's in an economically depressed environment or Beverly Hills – it happens at all levels. Those in the upper strata have access to high-end schools, high-end drugs, high-end rehab facilities, but they experience the same suicide rates.

One of the students wrote, "Pepper was good. He made me think a lot. Communication—I now seem to understand. You have to know about someone to communicate with him. Gangs, well, I always knew they were bad, but now I know why. He was smart about a lot. I saw him once before in Junior High School, but he wasn't as good as today. I can't wait for him to come back."

Another student wrote, "I think Pepper's talk was really good. I really like the part when he talked about communication. It made a lot of sense. But the best thing I think he talked about were gangs. Pepper's really a smart guy, but I think he was lying when he said he was 38." (The student thought I was actually in my early 20s.)

A different student wrote, "I think that what he said was very important, because I believe that it's true. Some people do give up only because they see that they're not getting it. I also think that me and you and all the people in this world have to care and love someone in this world. He was talking about parents. I felt sad, because I don't have my mother with me. I would like to care for my dad, but I don't think that he would ever care about me. If he did care about me, he would take me with him, but he didn't even bother to ask me. But I do have my little sister that I care about. I care for her and myself and my other family."

The principal wrote, "On behalf of Placer High School, I would like to thank you for your active involvement and participation in our recent Red Robin Week program. Your presentation during the rally and your efforts prior to it were extremely successful. I felt that our students are receptive to your method and your message."

STEP 1 OPENS ITS DOOR TO YOUTH

OUR initial thought when we opened Step 1 was that it would be for adults only—no youngsters. We didn't want to deal with children and their parents. We were opening a studio where adults were comfortable coming to dance, where they didn't have to dance with 12-year-olds. Well, that lasted for about a month! We quickly realized our real market came from parents and their families. Mary Wright said, "An adult-only dance studio is a great idea, but it only works on paper." Opening the studio to youngsters and their families ended up being the best business decision we ever made. That concept reflects what we stand for and always meant to stand for—to be inclusive.

Soon we realized that some kids couldn't afford lessons, so we set up "Youth Night," an evening of free dance lessons once a month, ending in a dance party. We felt students needed physical education and to have a positive hobby or a goal. All the staff got together, donating their time, and taught all types of dance to the kids ages nine to 19. The objective of Youth Night was for Step 1 to be a neighborhood youth center where kids could choose a healthy environment with creative arts, dancing, choreography and music versus drinking and hanging out on the streets in a less healthy environment.

Participants received two hours of free dance instruction followed by two hours of a dance party. Teens abide by our rules of no smoking, no drugs, no drinking—just exercise, dance, good music and fun. In order to participate in the dance party, they had to attend the free lessons. We'd turn down the lights and it was a party for over 100 kids. It kept them off the streets, and their parents were happy.

At Step 1, the studio is a place where discrimination in any form is not tolerated. Prejudice is a frame of mind taught by sick parents; children need to be taught otherwise and have examples put in front of them. Acceptance of all does not need to be stated here at the studio, because it is felt and experienced as soon as one enters the building.

This was part of our community outreach as a youth-friendly place, so they could experience and feel our intention of creating a safe, comfortable, non-judgmental place for them; aiding their growth and demonstrating community cooperation, as in "Community = Come Unity."

We knew we had to offer something that was appealing to youths. We built on this concept for several years. Even though the intention was focused on students and giving them positive choices, it was also for the teachers as well. Participation in these programs let them know that their role was much bigger than teaching a class, picking up their paycheck and going home. This was an opportunity to volunteer their time as part of their community service. It was acknowledging to themselves why they do what they do.

Volunteering their time, developing relationships with youths they wouldn't necessarily know otherwise, and keeping them safe was what made the instructors so valuable to the studio. The teachers looked forward to that night every single month. They were as excited about it as the kids.

In the beginning, other business owners would come in and say, "Are you sure you want to do that? They'll come in and wreck your place. They'll kick a hole in your wall." A hole in one of my walls versus a hole in somebody's head—I don't devalue my property, but it was worth taking the chance. We didn't have one hole kicked in the wall. We didn't have one student smoke a cigarette. We didn't have one person threaten to use drugs. We didn't have one fight.

We offered this program for several years. The program is not going on in the same way now, but opening our doors to teens is still part of our core fiber. The Saturday night activities laid the groundwork for Different Jam, a more structured program for students in grades 1-12. Using dance and discussion, I emphasized education and motivated young people to treat themselves and others with respect. Over time I spoke to individual classes and groups of almost 3,000 about drugs, teenage pregnancy, gangs, guns and violence.

ANTI-VIOLENCE, ANTI-GUN

I understand the Second Amendment of our Constitution granting citizens the right to bear arms. One thing I agree with the National Rifle Association about—and that's not my favorite group—is human safety. Safety is about the behavior behind the function of the gun. I believe guns kill people, just like knives kill people, just like cars kill people, just like cigarettes kill people. However, I believe that the behavior of people contributes to people killing people—not the gun per se.

On one hand, I understand the role guns play in our society. We have a culture that believes guns are the way we protect freedom, the way we stand up for the weak, and the way we protect the innocent. On the other hand, I am not pro-gun. I would rather we live in a society where we are respectful of our laws and law enforcement's most dangerous tool becomes pepper spray. Unfortunately, that's not the case.

Acknowledging we are going to have guns in our society, and we are going to make use of them, then let's talk about appropriate behavior and gun safety. Guns and cars are part of our society. Getting rid of guns is like saying we're going to do away with cars—that's not happening. So, let's talk about responsible driving; let's talk about defensive driving. Let's talk about responsible gun ownership.

When we talk about regulation and responsibility, there is less control over obtaining a gun than there is over getting a driver's license. Before a teen can drive, he or she has to attend a course in driver's education and train behind the wheel for a year—logging in driving hours with an adult followed by taking the driving test. Once you pass the test, other rules and restrictions come into play: you can't drive with other teenagers in the car, you have to have insurance, and you have to license your vehicle every year. There are all these limitations put on the driver to make sure he or she is safe in this contraption—this potential death machine. With guns, there is a five-day waiting period, and maybe a gun safety class is required, but it isn't a two-year process.

We have more opportunity to get caught in driving violations. How many times do you pass a sign on the street about gun safety? Yet, there are lots of signs about driving safely. Signs tell the driver safe driving speeds, warn of a dangerous curve coming, or road conditions like a pothole, or the danger of pavement being slippery when wet or icy. There are all these signs saying a car is a dangerous tool and we need to be aware of many situations. In fact, in 2015 a Duke University researcher concluded that owning an automobile is 80 percent more dangerous than owning a firearm, as it relates to others' lives.

Yet, I've never known a gun to improve anyone's health or quality of life. It seems somewhere as human beings in the United States we've lost our respect for human life. Too often, we've allowed violence and guns to become the answer. The bottom line is when dealing with stress, anger, confusion or frustration, loss of human life should never, ever be an option. I asked myself, "What is my part? How can I facilitate change?" My contribution to the solution is the CD "Enough is Enough: Guns" that provides our youth with increased awareness and motivation to explore options.

A "Different Jam"

THE "Different Jam" program for school-age children teaches fitness and self-esteem as an alternative to drugs and gangs. I designed the program in 1993 after continually hearing that the youth population is "at risk." As a former high school teacher, I know why students are at risk—they're confused and angry. They receive mixed messages from adults, television and music. They're told what's right, but shown what's wrong. When our young are at risk, the world is at risk. I was troubled by teen violence and a lack of structured activities for our youth.

"Different Jam" is a creative dance and motivational program designed to teach students respect for themselves and others, personal pride, self-esteem and sense of community. "At Step 1, Pepper's in his element: direct, thoughtful and passionate," relates his business partner Mary Wright. "Pepper is a teacher at heart and believes in the importance of educating kids to understand that we are all part of one family, despite differences in gender, race, age, religion or political opinions."

I received numerous awards for my work and commitment to the community. I have choreographed and co-directed several anti-drinking and driving commercials, which earned me the Attorney General's Award of Merit. My fitness programs for the physically disabled gained national attention and were featured in Self magazine.

Jane Hamilton, assistant principal at Placer High School, wrote, "I think you have made a vital contribution to our community. Your work with Sheri Graber and the Different Jam program has helped a lot of people, and has given direction and models to a lot of students in our community. I appreciate the difference you make."

It's difficult to teach students to generate their own self-confidence, but I'm strong-willed because growing up I watched friends come close to not surviving, and that has given me the insight to know when the youth I work with are endangered. I can listen to their feelings and help guide them to a more positive place. Sometimes I encountered difficult kids with gang signs on their faces who made a career out of hiding how they really felt. Breaking the ice with these kids and getting them to show their approval was extremely tough. Situations where I don't do this as well as I'd like force me to grow. I assess the situation and figure out how to approach and reach the students differently next time. I don't have all the answers, but I do have a good heart. I work hard to introduce the importance of fitness and wellness by serving as a positive role model for individuals of every age, ethnic persuasion and physical ability.

SERVING THE SPECIAL NEEDS POPULATION

I am known for my work with the special needs populations. By 1990, classes at Step 1 included dance and fitness for the physically disabled. I am certified by the National Handicap Society to teach fitness to the disabled population. I've served on the Governor's Committee for Employment of Disabled Persons and consult with other fitness professionals in the development of similar programs throughout California. Our "Fitness for Everyone" program includes those in wheelchairs and those who are hearing impaired.

I enjoy dancing and helping people progress in fitness so much that I think it should be available to everyone. I don't believe in cultural prejudices. There is a community of disabled people who we never see, and they should be able to participate. They should have the opportunity to move to music—they have a right to be fit. Most formal dance training and exercise studios don't accommodate disabled people. We work with quadriplegic, paraplegic, cerebral palsy, and muscular dystrophy students. In "Sit and Be Fit," we work on cardio stamina, muscle training, upper body strength and dance arm positions. We focus on their abilities, not their disabilities. We show them how talented they are.

I'm very visible promoting health in the wheelchair community. Our intent is to explore the movement inherent in four wheels and to combine that with the freedom and expressiveness of modern jazz. Long before it became a law, Step 1 was built with ramps to make the studio accessible to wheelchair users who learn to modify moves from a sitting position. This class is open to anyone who is not leg or foot mobile, so even injured athletes take the class. Able-bodied students come to class too; they sit down and work out. Able-bodied students are happy, because it has broadened their perspective and opened that channel of communication. Everyone is very comfortable working out together.

We also teach the blind and deaf. Our instructors have to be willing to work with people who have limited abilities. Blind students are taught to feel directions—six o'clock, twelve o'clock, three o'clock. For the hearing-impaired students, extra speakers are placed face down on the studio floor so they can feel the vibrations, and instructors give movement cues in sign language for our "Rhythm Workshop."

Alexa Yee was instrumental in helping bridge the gap between the hearing and hearing impaired community at Step 1. Yee is hearing impaired and also a signer with a strong desire to dance with music. Dancing to music was a dream she thought would never come true. She attended my rhythm class for the hearing impaired and was ecstatic to not only feel the musical vibrations through the dance floor, but through our creativity, learning other ways to sense vibrations. When she discovered tap dancing, it opened a new world for her. She could channel, direct, express and dissipate some of her boundless energy. She did not have to hear the music to dance; she made the music with her feet. The rhythm of the tapping became the music of her heart and soul.

I had always wanted to learn sign language and asked Alexa to teach me and the other three dance instructors. This led to a rhythm class for the hearing impaired. Rhythm is the first class, because it is the nucleus of music and dance. Alexa found she could feel musical vibrations by holding a balloon and feeling the vibrations reverberating through the floors. Alexa's once inconceivable dream became a reality; she can now dance to the beat of the music.

It was a little scary business-wise for us to venture out and provide these opportunities for people with disabilities. But in the end, we're all just people with abilities, and I wanted to help us all stretch toward our potential. In 1990, I received the Leadership Award of Excellence for my leadership and dedication to the fitness industry.

STEP 1 AS A PROFESSIONAL STUDIO

STEP 1 is a professional studio that is now the largest jazz academy in Northern California. Through word of mouth, it has developed a strong reputation in Los Angeles where teachers recommend Step 1 to dancers who are heading north. I am a demanding teacher. I expect a lot from my students, because I'm all about progress. That's just my style. I will say, "Again, do it again. That wasn't right. Do it again."

This strategy has paid off, not only for me but for our students. Many have gone on to professional careers to dance with Michael Jackson, Beyonce and other big names. All that talent comes from right here in Sacramento.

THE JABBAWOCKEEZ

THE Jabbawockeez dance team started dancing together at Step 1. They are an all male, hip-hop dance crew best known for being the winners of the first season of MTV's America's Best Dance Crew. They mention me as one of their mentors and inspirations.

It is amazing—these were just young street kids who wanted to dance, and by working hard fulfilled their dream. These weren't students who went to college or spent years in formal dance training. A couple of them were only in high school when they were with us at Step 1. The Jabbawockeez established their crew by wearing white masks and gloves. I initially worked with Jabbawockeez and took them into a more organized musicality. I taught them how to count, choreograph and teach. They became part of our staff, and from the studio went to the Hollywood audition. After winning the contest, they went on to perform internationally. In 2010, the Jabbawockeez debuted their own live stage show at the MGM Grand Hollywood Theater in Las Vegas and were the first dance crew to headline a show there. They moved to the Luxor in 2013 in a brand new, 850-seat theater. Step 1 helped facilitate their growth.

CHAPTER 9

My Lifestyle

WHILE I am co-owner of Step 1 and a dance/fitness instructor, I am also a choreographer, personal fitness trainer, licensed paramedic, nationally certified cardiovascular and aerobic instructor, motivational speaker and educator. I have been named trainer and spokesperson for the National Handicapped Sports and Recreation Association. There's no doubt my lifestyle is unconventional and I am an over-achiever!

MY TEACHING METHOD

THERE are people who are born to be teachers. They come to this planet to teach. I am one of them. Every bone in my body lends itself to teaching, and that's not just dance but also life's lessons. There is no way I could not teach. Teachable moments are something we come across daily, and I always embrace them.

I love being a teacher. My goal is to help my students—whether professionals or beginners, physically fit or physically challenged—strive to reach their ultimate vision, a sense of spirit, respect, health and happiness. My mission is to embrace, educate, enhance and empower others. But aren't we all teachers in some sense?

As a teacher I try to figure out the most effective ways to articulate Pepperisms to the students in my classes, my speaking audiences and people I meet. Information is not for me to keep; the ultimate goal is dispersion. If you have all the right information but can't share it, of what use is it beyond the personal?

It is up to the teacher to awaken joy in creative expression and knowledge. Hopefully, each of us has learned a few things along our journey in life. We can share this with our youths and other adults. My goal is: teach one, reach one. I have presented to youths in detention facilities, at school assemblies, and those who have walked into Step 1. I reach adults at fitness conventions, corporate trainings, through private consulting, and people I meet on the street. Those who enter my life, whether for a moment or for years, are the ones I am destined to share my talents and tools with while they are in my circle of energy. These are the ones I have the opportunity to reach. You, too, have the chance to touch the lives of people in your circle of energy and be a teacher to them.

We may lack confidence in our role as a teacher, but have the confidence that when we do our part and let God do the rest, everything works out fine.

A variety of classes are offered at Step 1 for all skill levels— beginning through professional, and all stages of life. I am committed to my students at the studio and in the master trainer classes I teach around the world. I am very demanding as a teacher. I truly care about my students in class and push all of them to be better and stronger. I never let people slide and be mediocre when I know they can do more.

"When he's teaching, things just 'pop.' It is a magical thing. He gets the very best out of people, and that's his gift. He only expects out of you what he is willing to give. His standards are high. He doesn't settle," explains Keith.

My dance and fitness style of teaching style is to use "add ons." I break things down to explain a technique and then the students do it. Then I go back and add on the next movement. That way it is easy for students to learn all the movements.

My breakdown goes deeper because of my technical knowledge of dance and the body. I learned anatomy from my medic training, and years of dance and choreography have added to my knowledge base. When I'm teaching fitness pros, I break down muscle involvement and placement necessary for toning and conditioning. I explain what our muscles are going to do to achieve a particular movement—how you're going to have to pull tighter or relax in a certain area. If lengthening of the leg is desirable, it is not just about pointing the foot. I am able to delve into and explain how the specific muscles are involved to achieve the desired effect. This combination of knowledge lets me know about training those with special needs—for asthmatics, I may give breath practice, or for the paraplegic, more arm movements.

As a teacher of teachers, I encourage others to be an overall positive role model. I instruct teachers about image; you have to look the part. You can't come into class with ballet clothes to do hip-hop. You need something—baggy shorts, a hat, or something—to give a little character to what you want to achieve.

As dancers, this concept of image involves how you are going to stand, how you are going to get on and off stage. Later, this transfers to how you are going to stand before the class and how the students are going to stand in class. In dance classes, the teacher may have students line up and go across the floor two at a time as the other students are watching. In my classes they are never allowed to stand around and just watch. They have to clap and look alive. Clapping as you are watching keeps you engaged and shows support for others. That is an important part of the classroom. When I have to stop a class and re-direct focus because someone is standing wrong or not getting the movements the first time, we do it again.

"Pepper will take your dancing or training beyond the expectations and limits you thought you had, to a higher performance," says Keith Goings. "We have this philosophy: you've got to do it – then do it again, do it right –then do it again, do it wrong – then do it again, do it, do it, and do it again. Repetition is our friend. When you reach perfection, you do it again, because you want to keep that level," says Keith.

When it comes to performing and teaching, I have an eye—not a critical eye but an intuitive one – for recognizing talent, for recognizing the "it" factor, and for developing both so they become more structured. I subconsciously know what people need, and I present it to them whether they are ready for it or not. They may not always understand that what I'm really telling them is just what they need. Sometimes they may be resistant to the message. In that way, I'm a little bit pushy, because people don't always know what they need. My responsibility is to relay the message and help them break through whatever barriers they are experiencing.

My students must be open to learning about life in general. I tell stories or share my experiences in what have become known as Pepperisms. Students may think, "Where's this story going?" But in the end, they find it comes full circle and is important for them or the class, or pertains to what they're doing and why they need to know something of importance. Choosing what to share and when to share it is often intuitive on my part.

Alisa Shubb, another long-time student, dancer and teacher at Step 1, says the following:

"When Pepper is speaking, you are hearing more than what is being said. He opens you up beyond basic information. He is telling you things that are deeper, that are really going to help you grow. In many ways he is strict and demanding, but he's cool and super fun, too! Pepper's teaching style is always on the cutting edge. At any given moment, his mind is creating his next direction. Whatever it is, it won't be just a trend but the foundation of something new. Being on the cutting edge is a rare talent. Some people are simply ahead of their time—but someone has to be the pioneer, and that's Pepper's role. Oftentimes, the information he is giving to people, whether it's in a dance form or fitness form, is new information.

For instance, the fitness classes we did years ago are still valid, but there was no organization of aerobics when Pepper was first teaching aerobics. He was doing new things based on the knowledge he had at the time, and they were the best workout classes you could attend. It turns out the things he incorporated were right as further information came to light. The fitness field said that's what all instructors should be doing—like meditating, breathing and relaxation being included at the end of classes. Over the years there are a lot of micro-trends that Pepper was already incorporating when the industry picked them up.

The main thing is that he brings other people along. He isn't just putting Pepper out there; he's bringing people along; he's bringing the team along; he's bringing the dance company along; he's bringing the studio along; he's bringing all the people who have had experiences like him along. He works really hard and then brings everyone along with him in his growth."

Jackie Anderson, a student for many years, says, "Pepper as a teacher is one in a million. He's just stellar. In his musicality, he is very talented. His choreography is imaginative, fun, creative, and ever-changing. He has the ability to get the very best out of people. Sometimes people are kicking and screaming when he demands so much of them, but they do it. He's a great instructor. I'm not a dancer, and that he can teach me to dance any kind of way is amazing. Pepper does have magic. He exudes it. There's something that comes from him that brings the best out in people. You get into his world, pulled in by his smile and his energy."

Janice Mitchell, a friend and student for nearly 30 years, adds the following:

"As a teacher, Pepper is powerful and dynamic. Magnetic. He loves the challenge of teaching the new student who has come for the first time, while meeting the needs of the advanced dancer in the same class at the same time, and everybody in between. He is that diverse as a teacher. And everybody feels they are getting his personal attention!

Pepper inspires people. He works with people of all ages. If they are 80 and want to take the class, or if they are disabled, he'll work with them. When I first started to take classes, the whole back row was wheelchairs. He touches the lives of everyone—not just young students. Yes, he does touch and reach a lot of the kids because of his hip-hop, and he's cool. One of his gifts is the ability to establish rapport with anybody. He's a role model, and he accepts that responsibility. Knowing Pepper has impacted my life. His biggest gift is teaching me discipline, not only in working out, but this has carried into other areas of my life.

Today, Pepper is gone every weekend somewhere conducting master classes to fitness instructors as a guest teacher. People in Sacramento don't realize the caliber of teacher he is or his international reputation. They take him for granted. I've taken his classes for 28 years and feel very fortunate. That says something about the caliber of teacher he is."

BETO PEREZ AND ZUMBA®

As a Zumba education specialist, I traveled around the world to train people to be licensed to teach Zumba. My direct connection to the Zumba organization is through Beto Perez, the creator and founder of Zumba. Perez tells this story of our first meeting:

"In 1994, I had the unbelievable opportunity to go to my first aerobics convention in Bogota, Colombia, where the fitness celebrity, Pepper Von, was presenting. I had the privilege to take one of his classes, and in the middle of his session, he invited me and my best friend, Walter, to join him on stage. I couldn't even sleep that night; I was full of joy and felt privileged for the opportunity.

Two days later, there was a meeting for some of the instructors, where Pepper was giving a speech about fitness and motivation. After a while Pepper asked if anybody had a question. I raised my hand and asked, while a translator helped me, 'If I have an idea about a different type of fitness class, what do I have to do to become a respected, well-known instructor like you and make people believe in my fitness program?'

Pepper's answer was exactly what I was doing at the time, and he ensured me that I was on the right path. He said: 'Who perseveres and is patient will make it far in life, and then the right moment will come in the right place.'

A lot of years went by, and I kept my thoughts and Pepper's advice always in focus. I believed in myself as an instructor and in my program. Now, years later, after Pepper's speech, I see the results and the success reflected in Zumba Fitness.

I invited Pepper to the 2011 Zumba international convention in Orlando, Florida. And we worked together on a video. I introduced him to all my students and instructors as my mentor and inspiration. I believe it is important that everyone knows that we all learn from each other and have a mentor who we learn a lot from, and in my case, this mentor was Pepper Von."

STEP 1 REUNION

ONE of the best times we recently had was celebrating the 25th anniversary of Step 1. All I had to do was ask a few people to help; people were willing to volunteer to put together this party. We found all kinds of old pictures. When people were contacted or heard about the party through Facebook and other social media, they were very excited. As it turned out, it wasn't an anniversary party—it was a reunion. All the people, from even before Step 1 started, came. It was very rewarding to reconnect with everyone. It seemed that no matter what, people eventually would orbit back into my life.

With so many students who keep coming back, you think they must care somewhat, but sometimes they aren't showing it by their actions in class. In teaching, we're dealing with a nebulous quality. When you are performing, the audience responds and claps, and you know you've succeeded. But as a teacher, you don't always know. You plant seeds to sprout in the future. You can't say you've achieved a certain quantitative level and are, therefore, successful.

When I lead a class, I set a certain standard. When that standard is not met, I question: Is there something I am not doing enough as a teacher? It affects me when I feel people won't let me teach them, when there is a wall of resistance. I'm thinking: if you won't do what I'm requesting, you won't grow. It becomes personal. I'm not selling a class, per se. My goal is to teach and empower. The classes, wherever and whatever they are, are my vehicles to reach that goal.

When all that happens at Step 1 rather than on the road, I am more affected. It is rewarding to know a 30-year, family-oriented business includes several generations of students, many of whom are now parents and bring their children for classes.

The teacher needs to recognize the contribution of his or her energy to the class, and always strive for his or her personal growth and development as well. I am always growing and developing, so my classes remain fresh because of the changes in me.

HEALTH, DIET AND REST

BALANCE is one of the greatest challenges for me in my life. Basketball coach John Wooden wrote in *Wooden—A Lifetime of Observations and Reflections On and Off the Court:*

"Balance is perhaps the most important word for a player or coach to keep in mind. You have to have emotional balance. You have to have physical balance. You have to have mental balance. Balance means keeping things in proper perspective, not permitting either excessive exuberance or dejection to interfere with preparation, performance, or subsequent individual behavior."

To me, as a performer, a philanthropist, a mentor, a father and a businessman, all these aspects of my personality require balance. Health, diet and rest are all about living a balanced lifestyle, too.

I made a conscious decision not to smoke, drink or do drugs when I was about ten years old. My parents' habits prompted this decision. I had seen the outcome from my family members. I was asthmatic, and it was hard for me to breathe around smokers. This was in the days when everyone smoked everywhere—even in the car with the windows rolled up. I hated smoking because I just couldn't breathe.

I would outgrow asthma to some extent years later through continuous activity when I was in the service. The thing about my type of asthma is that the bronchioles are so inflamed, you can't inhale, because you've exhaled very little, so there's only a little room for more air in the lungs. As a child, I spent many times in the emergency room in oxygen and mist tents, and had ephedrine shots.

I had grass-induced asthma, pollen-induced asthma, stress-in-duced—which means exercise-induced— asthma. I had to become more conscious of all my triggers, like wallowing in dried grass or being around people who smoked. As I grew, as an active person, my body began to adapt to the continuous activity to a point where I was able to control the episodes with the use of less and less equipment like inhalers. It's like a diabetic learning to control their diet and insulin. People would say I outgrew it, but that's not true. It is too simplistic of an explanation. I did it through years of training my body and mind. I don't think the doctors ever told my mother I should not go outside or participate in sports.

Recently I had asthmatic episodes—the first in many years. The initial one was shocking and sent me to the hospital. It took me by surprise and back to my childhood. Experiences like that are branded in your hard drive. My mind immediately spun out of control. Since then, I've had six episodes, but they weren't as shocking, because I knew what to expect and how to deal with the situation.

My not drinking is directly associated with childhood traumas because there was a lot of alcohol in my family. At a young age, I blamed the dysfunction on alcohol, and I hated that. Although most children don't even recognize the impaired functioning in their family, they ignore the cause, fight it, but don't transform it into a positive. I made a conscious decision against the contributing factors to my family dysfunction. I didn't want anything that contributed to the pain of my childhood to be a part of my adult life—ever! I locked that decision into my mind early.

YOUR BODY, THE ACTIVITY MACHINE

THE way you manage the activity machine that is your body affects everything—including your relationships and actions.

Managing your body is about health and wellness. Our body reflects our life on every level. As healthy or unhealthy as we are—physically, emotionally, mentally or spiritually—our body will tell our story, reflecting our history without our permission.

I compare our bodies to a car. The car represents something about us. Everyone knows what their car means to them. For some, it is a status symbol; for others, a sign of success or a sense of pride. For some, it must be a certain type of car, something they don't want scratched or dented. For others, it is just a way to get from point A to point B.

The car is an activity machine. The maintenance of one often parallels the maintenance of our body as an activity machine. We wake up in the morning and have an expectation that our body is going to get us through our day, without the drama of breaking down. Likewise, we wake up, go out to our car, put the key in, and expect the car to get us to our destination without drama. That's our hope. And yet when we hear a little sound under the hood that we know isn't right, we don't wait until the engine falls on the ground to look into the problem. We take it into a shop for maintenance as soon as possible, so the mechanic can take care of it. Yet, when we get some sign in our body, a pain, discomfort, or shortness of breath, we ignore it or say, "I'll just walk it off." We put off addressing the sign until something breaks down and we become incapacitated. We need to listen to our body and take care of it as an activity machine before that happens.

DIET

MY advice on diet and health is to educate yourself. I'm selective with my own diet in the sense that there are certain things I just don't like. It seldom has to do with health and is more about my food likes and dislikes. Fortunately, a lot of things I do not like are also not healthy. For instance, I don't like hard sweets like candies; I don't like hard cookies; I don't like coconut; I don't like peanut butter; and I don't like chocolate. I'm not a fruit pie type of person, either. I don't have to discipline myself to stay away from those things, and I'm fortunate in the sense I have a fast metabolism.

What do I eat in a typical day? Because my metabolism is so high, I consume 4,000+ calories a day. That is a lot of food, but I eat dense food, so I don't need a lot of food bulk. I can drink a protein shake, and that could supply 1,800 calories, making the calories add up fast. On the average, I drink maybe one shake a day. These days it's a green shake along with meals. I do moderation in meals—eating a little bit of everything. My blood type (O+) requires all types of food. In every meal, I try to get protein, carbohydrates and fats. Fats are important. Without good fats, your organs don't function well, including your brain.

I've gone extreme on occasion—like being a vegetarian. But there's not enough protein or calories in a vegetarian diet to meet my needs. I'm not a big fan of bread, seafood or mushrooms. I had to develop a taste for green vegetables. The body is an adaptive machine; you give it something often enough and that consistency breeds expectancy - your body requests it.

My laziness is found in food. I don't like to work to eat my food. I don't like meat with bones you have to chew around, or dealing with an ear of corn. That's why I don't eat chicken wings—if I have to gnaw on something, it's too much work.

There's no bad food - there are only foods that meet your needs or don't. First, I try to get my food using a knife, fork and spoon, not from a straw. The whole system of digestion—beginning with our jaw, our teeth and the enzymes in our mouth—is designed for us to chew food, digest it and break down what we consume into a usable form. If we are sucking down our calories, that is, drinking our meals, we are missing the entire digestive process. Even though I often include shakes with my meals, I try not to nourish my body from a supplement, trying instead to nourish it from a plate.

Diet, as with life in general, goes back to balance. I try to eat a balanced diet. I know in every meal there should be a balance. I know that not eating enough is not good. I know that eating too much food is not good either. I know I personally need a balance of carbohydrates and protein. Too much of one or the other is not balance and, therefore, does not produce the best energy level for my body as a high-performance energy machine. It has taken time to figure out what works best for my activity machine at different stages in my life.

I encourage people to educate themselves by listening to their body. When we listen to others—in this case, the latest fad in eating—chances are they are trying to sell us something. By attempting to separate us from our money, they are separating us from our health. They will separate us from our money at any cost, and that cost is our health.

I'm big on health, food, and movement education (in the form of dance or exercise), and then consistency. You can't build consistency over a short period of time; it must be a lifestyle change, and be a lifestyle that works for YOUR life. It may be a great lifestyle for someone, but if it doesn't work for your life, move on. Flexibility to adjust as needed is important.

Someone may ask, "What do you think about supplements?" I'm not opposed to supplements. As a matter a fact, I am a fan of them, but they are called supplements for a reason. If, due to your lifestyle, you are not getting what your body needs from the food you consume, then supplements are better than nothing. You may be at a point in your life where you can't get all the nutrients you need from the food on your plate, so taking supplements is a good idea, but eat a balanced diet first.

I teach people there is no such thing as a good diet or a bad diet. Instead, there is an effective or ineffective diet for you. An ineffective eating plan for you may be highly effective for another person. So, it's not a bad plan, just not a good plan for you. I am fortunate enough to know my health needs, and I supply my body with what it needs. It's like your car; you choose the grade of gas that's best for the engine to run efficiently. For some engines, it's high octane; for others, regular grade will do.

My lifestyle is simply not conducive to spending a lot of time preparing meals. I wear a lot of hats each day: athlete, business owner, parent. I don't have time to shop, steam vegetables, or juice fruit. And I know I'm no different than a lot of people living in this fast-paced world. But good nutrition is a key ingredient in a healthy lifestyle, along with exercise and the proper amount of rest. Balancing all three is difficult, especially for busy people.

THE MIND-BODY CONNECTION

I struggle with my own physical challenges. I've had my hips replaced. Usually, my first reaction, because I was a medic, is to go the conventional medical route. However, I am very open to the mind-body connection. I believe in both allopathic medicine and complementary healing therapies like massage and reflexology; I know they work well together. During the healing process of my convalescence I had to accept the help of others. The fact that I have a quick recovery process is a direct result of my spiritual philosophy, exercise and diet. My friend Janice notes, "He gives everything in himself, sometimes to his physical detriment. He went to a special orthopedic hospital in Oakland to have a benign tumor removed in a muscle near his groin and came back to work quickly. He had hip replacement surgery and took very little time off. When he had knee surgery and was very ill from an infection, he could barely walk with a cane, and he was back teaching right away. That is Pepper, but we were all worried."

Throughout my life, I have had to rely on my determination, perseverance, and courage, coupled with incredible hard work applied to each opportunity that has presented itself in my life. I think it is important to share with my students what I went through, and what I learned in the process. For instance, people knew I had knee surgery—they knew I almost died—but by sharing my journey they are able to understand something more they can take away for themselves from my experience. In my training, I talk a lot about components of that experience, but my family in Mississippi has no idea what I went through.

STARTING MY DAY

I'M often asked: How do I begin my day?

My goal is to start happy and end happy. Happy is kind of an elusive word. When I say happy, I mean what makes me feel good. Happy for me is a feeling of joy. This is not contentment, because to me contentment feels like a gray area – not angry or unhappy but I don't have joy. A lot of people exist in that gray area, but I choose not to. That's why everyday I make the decision to be happy.

Daily, something is going to lead my parade, and I have a choice what that's going to be. Life may lead to the left or the right during the day, but in the morning, I decide what's going to lead, and that's happiness.

This is about how I'm going to allow myself to feel; it's not necessarily about accomplishing a task. I can let myself feel out of sorts, or in a bad mood, or a little angry with my body because my knee hurts and the healing process is taking too long. I can make these feelings legitimate or say to myself, "I know this part of my journey doesn't feel good, but considering the other alternatives and what other people are experiencing, I'd take my challenges any day." Being grateful works its way back into my attitude and I feel blessed. My life isn't perfect, but I am grateful. I let this energy of gratitude lead the parade for the day in the way I feel.

The only consistency in my day, and what I incorporate more now, is the saying that I want to feel good that day. Feeling good and in balance incorporates feeling mentally, emotionally, physically and spiritually good. For me, one leads into the other. If I am uncomfortable physically or out of balance, I tend to be out of sync with the other parts of myself as well. I really have to focus my energies and know that I really am fine, that all is well in spite of thinking, as a physical specimen, that life doesn't feel too good right this second.

Beyond this, I'm not consistent in how I begin my day—I don't have a strict regimen or routine. To me, each day is unique and brings its own way as to how I go into that day. Days when I don't have to meet professional responsibilities are different than days when I do. The bottom line is that each day I choose happiness and then follow what I am led to do.

For decades my mantra has been: Do not let me miss the opportunity to be a miracle in someone else's life today. That doesn't change. When I say that, I really do look for opportunities throughout the day to make life better for others. And there are always many such opportunities. Doing good could have been something as simple as wiping up in a public restroom so the person behind me doesn't have to experience a mess. Whatever the opportunity is doesn't matter. The question to be answered is: Is the world a better place for my having been in it today?

From this morning mental inventory, I get started with my day.

I need light, so I tend to immediately look for sunshine by throwing open the curtains.

On the other hand, I don't need silence. I don't need to go to a quiet place on a regular basis. That's not the way I connect with my day, Spirit or myself. Sound vibration is energy, just like sunlight is a vibration. Both help me to plug myself into the universe. Therefore, I need some kind of background noise—white noise. This gives me the sense that energy is starting to move. I might turn on the television, whether or not I watch it, turn on the radio, or turn on music. Everything in my day flows from there.

ENDING MY DAY

I end my day the same way I begin, but in reverse. I usually have some type of sound around me. I'm not one of these people who can say, "time for bed," and be able to shut their mind off and fall asleep. Maybe I'll watch a little TV. Overall, regardless of what is involved, when it is time to end the day, when I close my eyes and go to sleep, I want to be in a state of peace.

To achieve peace, I reflect on what has happened during the day. I do a daily inventory. Going back to my mantra, I ask: "Okay, what did I do?" I review and acknowledge my opportunities and ask myself whether or not I fulfilled them or feel good about them. This goes back to who I am, what my calling is, what my job is, because these traits are validated every single day, whether they involve professional commitments or personal ones.

I start by acknowledging opportunities, where I felt I fulfilled my mantra. That makes me feel good about myself. I end by feeling grateful that I made it through the day. I acknowledge that some who started their day didn't make it. I ask whether I was relevant that day and how did I make a difference? Such reflection doesn't mean was I perfect. There are often things, methods, or processes I went through in the day where I think, "I would do things a little differently next time." Or the outcome would have been more brilliant if I had approached a situation differently or used other words.

Reflection in hindsight is to see where my energies are at the end of the day. No one but me knows if I was off that day as I smiled so much my face hurt. If there was somebody in my day I pissed off, then I pray for the person even if the other person doesn't know and is not aware of my prayer. They don't need to know—it's my thing, not theirs. The process of reflection and forgiving myself brings me joy and happiness, because to upset that person was not my intent.

I've found throughout life people will make you mad, disrespect you and treat you badly. I've learned to let Spirit deal with the things other people do, because hurt and hate in my heart will consume me. The goal of my life is to be happy, and it is counterproductive to harbor bad feelings toward others. So I practice forgiving anyone who has hurt me: first, because that person may not even know they hurt me, and second, because some people come in your life as blessings while others come in your life as lessons. The key is to forget what hurt you, but never forget what it taught you. Third, my attitude hurts me, not them. It does not bring me happiness. My goal is to end the day with peace and joy as I go into sleep.

A lot of this process is not step-by-step consciousness. But if I corral my various thoughts, this is where I end up. It is not a linear process for me—my thoughts may flip to one thing, then another, and back to the first one. I give myself permission to let my mind drift.

If my head is racing and the day has been very creative and ideas have been flowing, then I need to slow down my thoughts. There are times where I have to go more into a phase of meditation to calm my mind down because, for me, when my creative motor runs, it runs hard and fast.

To calm my mind, the first thing I do is acknowledge the creative process as a gift from God. The only reason my mind is running is because there is something within it I need to discover. I don't go into denial or become irritated that it's inconvenient to get up and write down what comes to me. I get up and record it, so it isn't lost. I've literally come to the end of my day with some choreography in my mind, not because of the demand of a deadline, but because creativity is bringing motion pictures to my mind right then. I don't know if they will be there tomorrow morning if I don't record them.

Overall, I try to end my day by finding peace in the way my day went. All this may sound complicated, but it isn't. It is all about letting my mind flow. I am not trying to force anything into a specific structure. I am open to receiving whatever the message is; the important thing is to listen and receive the message.

A minister friend of mine says, "Pay attention to what you pay attention to." In other words, pay attention to what won't leave you alone. When I talk about the voice of God, I mean that when your "soul" comes knocking on the door, don't check the peephole; just open the door! When the voice of God comes calling, don't check the caller ID—just answer the phone. There are times at the end of the day when my creativity is going, and I have to flow with it, and to accept what's recorded is perfect, not perfection. We're just like a megaphone—it is not our voice. It is from God through us.

SLEEP

I expend a lot of energy during the day. As a fitness professional, I know the value of recovery. The sleep I need depends on what's happening in my day, what my energy needs are. Again, it can be likened to how much gas you need to put in your car. It depends on where you are going. Some days I can function extremely well on four hours of sleep. But those were a good four hours of deep sleep. Or I can get in bed and sleep eight to ten hours and wake up feeling exhausted. My tendency is to function best on six to eight hours.

I don't like alarm clocks. To me, it's a jarring, artificial way to start the day. My mind has a built-in sense of time. I set my alarm and wake up on my own five minutes before it is set to go off and shut the alarm off. Sometimes, if I wake and it doesn't feel like it's time or I don't have any pressing need to be up—which is a luxury—I may drift back to sleep.

GROWING OLDER

NEVER regret growing old: it's a privilege denied to many. A 14-year-old who is taught about healthy living and choosing happiness doesn't care about turning 38. You find 38-year-olds who have never been taught the concepts of healthy living and they fear turning 39 – they are a mess and angry at the world. They see life as slipping away from them and live in fear and insecurity. There is a difference between the things we learn in life and the things we learn in school. In school, our lessons are bits and pieces of knowledge, then we live it; in life, we live it, then learn lessons through experience or the college of hard knocks. We only have the present day to live. Let us spend time wisely while we learn to enjoy life more and worry less.

Growing older, which is different than growing old, means the wine is getting sweeter. It means our Rolodex of life has more information in it based on experience. We have survived up to this point, and we look back and ask: "What gives us value? How are we and our lives relevant?"

Embrace growing older gracefully. Age brings freedom. Learning not to care what others think, expressing ourselves any way we want, having opinions, gaining emotional wisdom and achieving spiritual understanding are the things that set our soul free.

We can say, "I wasted the best 20 years... "And I'd say, "Hold on. Look back, reflect, and ask yourself what gives all that time value?" The only things that give life value are the lessons, which are synonymous with wisdom, information, age and experience. So, even in this youth-oriented culture, one need not fear getting older. Growing older is literally a gift.

SOUP OF LIFE RECIPE

MY Soup of Life recipe has nothing to do with food. My answer to life is simple—Live. My recipe is also simple. You need good nutrition to fuel your body. Eat "real," healthy, organic food—if possible. You need to move. Get lots of exercise—being fit contributes to being more productive. Get plenty of rest. Rest refreshes and heals your body. Have a positive attitude based on optimism and confidence. Set a goal. Plan to find your role in life by discovering what feeds your soul, not necessarily what feeds your wallet, and utilizes the talents you were born with.

Our biggest responsibility in life is to maximize our greatest potential. Yet, one of the tragedies of life is living the physical, mental or emotional plan of someone else's life, or the life that someone else thinks is right for you, rather than living our own truth. The consequence of not living our own truth is usually a life of unhappiness. It takes courage to live life, to be all you can be, and do all you are here to accomplish. You are unique, and there are things you are here to do that no one else can do as well. Finding yourself and your path is a lifelong challenge.

CHAPTER 10

Up Close and Personal

I believe that part of the journey of my great-grandfather, my grand-mother, my mother, our ancestors who have passed on—this whole host of people—is to make sure that our destiny is achieved. At their level of universal existence, they can't allow us to slip off the edge and have our destiny hanging in limbo so we have to come back around and do it again. I believe there are all these spiritual entities watching over us, but not judging us. The answer to many intangible, unanswerable questions regarding events that happen to us are explained when we say, "I don't know how that happened or how I got through that experience, but I did through the grace of God."

Whether we speak of our spiritual ancestors or guardian angels, they are the same spiritual guides nonetheless. Nothing is separate; we're all talking about the exact same thing, just using different words.

There is no one book that I can point to that encompasses what I believe, nothing that says exactly who I am. I keep reading. I know the Bible—back to front—from being a Southern Baptist and the catechism of Catholic school. We can question what we read and decide if it's a truth for us right now in our lives.

I read for inspiration. On a flight, I won't be reading just to read, but to learn. I'd rather take a nap than read to just be reading. Rest can be a productive use of time. I read for purpose, for information, for content, to make me think and for validation. There is always a purpose to my reading.

Books will always be in my life. All the time I have to be learning and sharing other people's experiences that they write about in their books. On my coffee table, there are self-help books containing empowering information on things that matter to me: books that talk about healing, spiritual concepts, communication, relationships, personal peace and personal power—the answers to life's questions. Enlightening information comes in through books on dance, fitness and health.

MY SPIRITUAL LIFE

MY mission is to unify people's hearts, to encourage them to have more fun. I help people realize, appreciate and be all they can be in each given moment. I make no bones about being spiritual.

My spiritual pursuit is very important. I don't know how or when I realized this. I'm not sure we control when we get this awareness. There wasn't one awakening moment when the light just shined in my life—Spirit has always been a companion along my way.

I was always able to integrate being raised both Southern Baptist and Catholic into my spiritual life without conflict. And I have never been separated from that influence. A lot of the morals and standards I received from both have been woven into my life. The spiritual life contributes to my moral life. Being who I am, I would probably be on the straight and narrow without influence from these outside sources, but I have felt divinely or spiritually guided in the opportunities that have come into my life. Once we are aware of Spirit working in our life, we may make the choice to follow it or not.

I am a passionate person. What I am passionate about, what brings me joy, and what makes my heart sing are all the same. Life is too short not to enjoy everything I do. I commit time, energy, emotion and resources to what I am passionate about. Then I look forward to feeding the nucleus of my soul and bringing it joy through my actions. Time, energy, emotions and resources are the four commodities I have to work with, and they are too precious to squander.

I'm at that point in life where the answer to life is really simple. It is one word, and that is Love. Finally, you get to that point in life where you can say, "Oh, now I see how that experience has played out." Understanding my role, I can appreciate and surrender to it.

How can I not smile every day? My heart is happy, and I realize it's my choice. My soul is happy, and it's my choice. What I do with my body is happy, and that's my choice, too. I am passionate about life itself, and the things I do are how I express my passion. There are avenues for me that make me grateful. I am truly blessed and grateful.

Being blessed does not mean life is always easy or there aren't challenging opportunities for me. However, life is too short not to enjoy everything I do, so I choose happiness.

GOD/SPIRIT/HIGHER POWER/SOURCE OR VOICE WITHIN

BY whatever name you call it, Spirit is within you.

My mission is to help unify people's hearts and create community. I encourage all of us to have more fun, to realize and appreciate the moment, and to be all we can be in every given minute.

I make no bones about being spiritual. I have felt divinely or spiritually guided and grateful for the opportunities that have come into my life. It doesn't matter what name we use: Spirit, God, a Higher Power, the Still Quiet Voice, the Universe or the Source, we are all referencing the same thing. Once we are aware of the ways Spirit works in our life, we can make the conscious choice to follow.

I've found that people don't give Spirit a chance to act in their life. We tend to want to control everything. But the results of events that happened in my life wouldn't have happened without Spirit stepping in.

Spirit's time is not our time, so we need to first ask in our prayers or meditation for what is in the highest interest of all involved. Secondly, we must allow Spirit time to work, not demand immediate results, and find the patience to wait. Patience is a valuable commodity.

Epictetus (55-135 A.D.) wrote, "Nothing great is created suddenly, any more than a bunch of grapes or a fig. If you tell me that you desire a fig, I answer you that there must be time. Let it first blossom, then bear fruit, then ripen."

What's in the hard drive of our mind didn't pop in there overnight – it was built program by program. We've had to learn to reconfigure or translate the information that's in our hard drive so it works for us. At the right time, all the information stored is translated and produces in us an "ah ha" moment.

There have been hard times in all our lives. I've sat in a rental car overlooking the ocean and had thoughts of suicide. To be grabbed out of that moment of human weakness and hear a quiet voice within saying, "Not yet," was Spirit talking to me. In the end, this experience was transformed into a story, a tragedy meant to be shared with others so they know they aren't alone, and someone else has been where they are.

There are people who have near-death experiences but come back into their bodies because it isn't their time. We might not necessarily have that exact experience, but the same process of our life being grabbed from disaster. We can all be given a pad of paper and list how many times, if things in our life had gone one inch differently, we wouldn't be here right now. There are many such incidences. Only by the grace of God are we still here, because it wasn't our time, and there are unfinished things only we can do.

There is Spirit-being and human-being. When we choose human-being that's when we suffer the consequences, when we suffer the most. When we learn to choose the spiritual path, when we surrender and stop trying to control the moment, that's when life seemingly flows effortlessly.

The purpose of life, at least from a spiritual perspective, is not physical survival, per se, but rather the evolution and elevation of our spiritual awareness—of our soul. How many times have you heard we are spiritual beings having a human experience? This goes back to having free will and choice. As infants, we came into the world neutral—a blank canvas. No matter how well-intentioned our parents, society, culture or religion was, our neutrality gets painted over. We need to understand that some things happened in our life where we didn't act in the best interest of ourselves or others. The Bible says that Jesus came and wiped the slate clean again. He said, "I'm not going to hold you accountable, because you didn't know what you didn't know. I'm going to take my eraser and give you the opportunity to do it a different way. And I'll continue to erase your errors and forgive you. You eventually have to get the lesson."

If you want to see God, open your eyes to the people, places and things around you.

TOOTIE'S DEATH

MY mother, Tootie, was in and out of the hospital for years before she passed in 2002. I was managing her affairs long distance, and flew back and forth many times from California to Mississippi whenever the family called me home, thinking she wouldn't make it through the night. In the end, she was in a care facility, though she fought being in one, and was very opinionated about not liking the care. But we had no other choice. None of us in the family were in the position to give her the care she needed.

The last conversation between Tootie and me was different from all the others we'd had. She wasn't aggressive or intimidating. She was on life support and had tubes everywhere. Having been a paramedic, I knew the stages in the dying process, but I couldn't make the decision to pull the plug ending her life.

In the room with her after my family left, I massaged and used reflexology on her feet to assist her into the space of love and peace, a place that was so uncommon for her. Then I sat beside her, holding her hand, and asked her to squeeze it if she wanted to go, if she was tired and wanted to leave, if she was ready, if she had done and said all she wanted to in this life.

At this point, she couldn't talk. Her eyes were closed, and she didn't squeeze my hand. She turned her head away, opened her eyes, and stared into space, saying nothing. She then closed her eyes, and the expressions crossing her face were as if she was reliving traumas; sometimes it was a frown and sometimes a slight smile. Tears ran down her face and her eyes flickered. I made sure I didn't interfere. I just sat there silently being with her and holding her hand, wondering how I was to interpret what her tears meant and how I was supposed to respond. After about twenty minutes—it seemed like hours—with her eyes closed, she squeezed my hand. Did her squeezing answer the question I had asked a while ago or mean something else? I didn't know. But in the miracle of the moment, I knew this was the end of an era—a rebirth for her. In this fragile state, I saw the spirit of who she truly was—the person she was before she became angry and bitter, began drinking, intimidating others. I knew her as an innocent soul.

Though I had witnessed many deaths before, witnessing her life journey at the point of transition was a gift to me. She was returning to the state of love, to the first moment of life here on earth as an innocent soul. In that moment I understood that ultimately, the intent of our journey here is a return to love—whether this is on our deathbed, in some other point of our life, or in another life.

There was only one time in my life – when I was leaving for the military – that my mother looked me in the eye and, recognizing she had no power over me or my life, her control having come to an end, saw me for who I was. Now it was my time to see the spirit of her as she was. I will take that insight with me forever.

I kissed her goodbye and don't remember driving home—some 60 miles away. I talked to the family at home and told them we'd all go visit her again in the morning. Later that night, the hospital called and said she had passed away. I waited until morning to share the news of her transition with my dad and my sisters.

HEAVEN

IN my mind, there are two types of heaven. To clarify the term heaven, it is not a plane of existence in an afterlife. Heaven is synonymous with such attributes as joy, wellness, light, compassion, peace and balance here on earth. These are the attributes we have mastered which make us successful in a spiritual way as we apply them to daily living in our present existence. True success is being better than our previous self of yesterday and maximizing our greatest potential. We are called to do what we do best, and do it to the very best of our ability every day.

My mission this time around in life is to help people get closer to heaven here on earth. As I've already shared, I start every day with the mantra, "Do not let me miss the opportunity to be a miracle in someone's life today." You don't have to be brilliant, rich, beautiful or perfect to make a difference in someone's life. You just have to care enough to be there for them. Care enough to respect people's beliefs and feelings because even if it doesn't mean anything to you, those beliefs and feelings could mean everything to them. There comes a time when just "being," rather than "doing," is helpful.

When I was born and my assignment– my destiny – was given to me, everything I needed to accomplish that destiny was also given to me, or would become more developed in me as I grew, so I could help others get closer to heaven. And where I leave off, when I leave this world, someone else will take over and keep this going. I fulfill my mission by being of service. Those people who need to be touched by the reason I was born will find me. They will be in my audience. They're going to be in my classes. They're the person who steps on my foot at the supermarket and I end up in a conversation with.

Our mission is different from day to day. Our strategy has to be different from day to day. Our audience will be different from day to day.

Recognizing this means being more conscious of the need for flexibility within myself. Accepting this flexibility is a whole different component. And trusting it is another big component. And then teaching it is the next step. It is hard for me to teach what I don't trust. It is hard for me to trust something I don't accept. And it is hard for me to accept something I don't see the value of it once I'm conscious of it. I have already accepted I am a teacher. I've always known of this plan, felt this plan, or known these other dimensions already have been in place, and it makes it easy for me to be comfortable stepping in front of people and talking from my heart.

I am willing to teach the willing. That doesn't mean I will reach everyone, but I'm willing to do what I have been sent to this place right now to do. I am willing. I didn't design it; I didn't create it. I can't own it, because it's on loan to me. I don't control anything.

POWER AND CONTROL

OUR kryptonite is our illusion that we control things. Now, if you think you are in control, I'll give you the benefit of the doubt: all you have to do is show me. I challenge you to demonstrate it in one simple way. And as easy as this sounds, I haven't had one person yet establish they are in control!

THE TIDE

OF all the natural forces on Earth – wind, fire, and water – water is the most powerful. It can chisel a rock; it can rust steel. Let's go to the coastline in our imagination and face the water to meet this dynamic force called the tide up front and personal.

Standing in front of the tide, let's spread our legs as far apart as we can. Then spread our arms as wide as possible. Now, when the tide comes in I want you to stop it. When you do that, I will acknowledge you are in control. When you stop the tide from coming in, I will believe you can control all things. When it comes in, let's then turn around and stop it from flowing back out. For some reason, no one's done this yet.

Since right away we've established you and I aren't in control, let's talk about this idea in more detail. Let that tide be synonymous with God or a higher source, which for now, we'll just call "a powerful force." Let our life be the beach and accept this powerful force comes in whenever it feels like it and we can't stop it, and it leaves some things on the beach that weren't there before.

This force brings things into our life—people, places, opportunities and other elements. We don't have any control over what it brings. We tried to stop it, but we couldn't. When the tide goes back out at its own discretion, sometimes it leaves very valuable things. It could have brought shells with pearls. But, on the average, what does it bring? It brings rusty cans, funky seaweed, things that don't look good, taste good or smell good. In reality, the tide has brought items disguised as opportunities and left it up to us to discover their importance. We can't control what is left, but how we are going to relate to it… that's what we can control.

In life, we don't deal the hand, the tide does. We can only play the hand we're dealt. Let's not focus on the hand but on how we play it. It is up to us to determine the value of what we find. The question is: How are we going to incorporate what has washed up on the beach into our life. Are we going to use it, or give it away so that it benefits others? Are we going to consider it garbage?

We soon come to understand that very often it is all about perspective. We look at the stuff and think, "What garbage. This stinky old piece of driftwood—it's just an old stick with moss on it. Get rid of it!" But someone else comes along, sees the same piece of driftwood, and says, "I've never seen anything like this. The wood has been carved by the water and the rocks it struck on its way to this beach. That makes it extremely unique. It is like a snowflake; there is not another one like it in the existence of the world." The person who sees something special and valuable in the piece of driftwood takes it home, cleans it up, shellacs it, puts it on a plaque, and hangs it on the wall where it can be seen every day. All who see it claim, "That's gorgeous; it's beautiful." It is all about perspective. It is the same piece of driftwood we thought was ugly and wanted tossed in the garbage. Now we say, "It's wonderful what the tide brought up onto the beach."

The tide comes into our life, up on our beach, and leaves opportunities for us. Then it goes out when it decides, not when we decide. It takes things away with it—perhaps different things that are important to us—and we shout "NO." But we can't stop it. If we haven't learned this lesson the first time we were at the beach, the same opportunity presents itself again, perhaps in a different form.

People come into our life and leave our life; people die or they move away, because the purpose they needed to serve in our life is over. We scream, "NO!" We think, how are we going to function without them in our life? Who will love us? Well, it's not about us. The tide brings people, places, and things into our life. But it isn't really about us, and the tide says, "Sorry, Charlie," and takes people, places, and things away. It may be painful, but everything orchestrated is in perfect order. It's a lesson in letting go and trusting the process.

When we don't learn the lesson the tide brings in, it will come back to us again and again. For life is 10% about what happens to us; the other 90% of the outcome is about how we think and feel about what we're experiencing. All we have is perspective, acceptance and "I can" or "I will." The goal is to have a willingness to move forward. All through my life, people have come into my life and were there to teach me, and to help me move closer to heaven.

It took me a long time to develop and articulate this story of the tide, but I felt this concept early in my life. Trying to control the tide gives me something to illustrate the concept that God is in charge. I like to use this scenario to explain to people the concept of surrender: there is a power greater than we are. Understanding what our gifts are and how they come, what their purpose is and how to live in peace all comes from knowing we don't have control. For some people, this story helps them grasp these concepts, concepts they may never have thought of before.

LIVING OUR DREAM

BECAUSE life is not predictable, living our dream is being able to just show up on the spot and improvise a response to what's going to happen next. Yet we try to be in full control of everything that happens to us. We have heard that the important thing is to know the difference between the 10% of what happens to us versus the 90% of what we think about what happens to us. We need to ask ourselves the question: "What do I think about how I feel?" And, "How do I feel about what I think about how I feel?"

Now, if 90% of the outcome is going to be determined by what I think and feel about where I've been or where I am, and my thinking is going to influence my action or reaction to what I am experiencing, I'd listen to my thinking!

However, our attitude does not give us the right to spew our self-doubt onto other people. Never be the cause of somebody's bad day. As we live our dreams every single day, we have the opportunity to contribute or be a miracle to someone else. Often, we are so caught up in our own life we miss these opportunities. When we start our day with an attitude of God—if we start our day with an attitude of compassion, love, creativity, sensitivity, and non-judgment—then we won't miss our opportunity to be a miracle in someone else's life.

ADVERSITIES

NOW you might ask yourself: "What about the bad days? What about those challenging days of struggle, suffering, pain and discomfort?"

Adversity is a word I use instead of struggle. We all have adversity. We have allowed the world to teach us how to suffer. But to me, adversity is synonymous with accumulating information, lessons and education. As we grow older, I think we need to learn to have perspective on what "is." Adversity serves a higher purpose—it is an advanced state of learning. Adversity is God's university. Adversity, struggle, and discomfort exist to promote our evolution as a spiritual being and usually force us in a new direction. Adversity provides us the opportunity to grow and learn within the challenges we face. It is our opportunity to learn, to be educated about something that if we'd written the script, we'd say, "Oh, no, I'm not writing that in, because that's going to bring some suffering. That's not going to smell good, taste good, sound good, feel good. I don't want to go there. I just want the comfortable, easy, fun way, even if I learn nothing."

Well, destiny disagrees. In order for us to grow, in order for us to learn, some of what comes to us is not going to feel good. And that's okay. What gets us through is our attitude about those experiences. Now, we can go through life kicking, biting, scratching, screaming, and guess what? At the end of the day, we are still going to end up where destiny says we're supposed to be.

That being the case, we might as well change our attitude. Once we, with passion, decide to understand and accept our destiny, then we will stop spending the rest of our life trying to force a round peg into a square hole. We will give our life up to the Universe, to God, saying, "What is it You want me to be? How many lives do You want me to touch, and in what way? I surrender, because I understand the only power I have is that which I exercise over myself." Then we show up with a great, positive and mighty attitude. Because it is the attitude that really determines the altitude we reach. Our goal in life is to be closer to heaven tomorrow than we are today. That's our goal. And I can guarantee you if you let your attitude lead you, everything else is going to fall into place, and at the end of the day, you will be where you want to be, and you will have touched the hearts and souls of many.

REGRETS

I have matured into not doing regrets as a way of identifying lessons. Regret is kind of a caption that we stamp on experiences that keeps us in a fear-based element. We must have experiences to have regrets, and if those experiences are uncomfortable—they didn't feel good, taste good, smell good, sound good—they still have value. Sometimes, we have to go through the experience to see its value based on what it has contributed to our destiny. I am thankful to see the outcomes of the choices I've made. Those experiences could have been stamped as regrets, but they have contributed to my being successful today and in the future, so they are valuable. And it's a choice to see life this way.

The only way life works is living through heart. I think that's the answer to our problems and what I attempt to do every day. My grandmother told me to leave a place better for my having been there. Everything I do—all of it—is all about my leaving the world a better place than when I came. My goal is to help all students strive to reach their ultimate vision, with a sense of spirit, respect, health and happiness.

CARING AND COMPASSION

I seemed to have been born with compassion that I carried with me into the military. My experience in the service has nothing to do with how I relate to the troubled minds of the homeless, especially veterans

I meet today. Whether my sense of compassion was influenced by my environment and the civil rights movement so that I see and react to mistreatment and injustice, I don't know. There is a part of me that just naturally sees beyond the physical to the spirit of the person. I feel a responsibility to make life better for others. This often has meant organizing a fundraiser to benefit individuals or foundations, or simply taking the time to listen. As busy as I am, I take the time to listen. If I promise to do something, I will. My word is gold.

MY FAMILY LIFE

I don't have a traditional family structure. My immediate family is composed of Kim Goetz, Mary and Kenna Wright, Janice Mitchell, her kids and grandkids, my daughter Gabby and her two girls, and Corina. They don't see me as a celebrity. They know me well—the good and those not-so-good parts we all have in our make-up. We're all very loyal to each other. When it comes to celebrating holidays, I am often with them.

"When you meet Pepper, your family becomes his family," says Greg King. "The same that he'd do for his family he'll do for yours. Not because you ask him, but because that's where his heart is. Once you come into his world, your family becomes his family. He may forget your name, but he won't forget your face or what your character is as a person. He has the gift to know who you are once he meets you."

My three "daughters"—Gabby, Kenna and Corina—have all come into my life differently and at different times. Yet, all three girls would stand up at my funeral and claim, "That's my dad."

Kenna is my daughter through being adopted as a baby by Mary. Gabby is my biological daughter, and Corina is my surrogate daughter. Kenna's mom and I never dated. I never dated Corina's mom; she only knows me through my association with Corina. Corina and Gaby were friends. In high school and college, I stepped up and filled the role of Corina's dad to inspire her, support her, and encourage her. Seeing her need, I could not have not stepped in. Only Gabby's mom and I dated. This blessed relationship brought us a miracle gift named Gabrielle.

Suffice it to say they all have different stories because they came into my life differently, which also means the journey I've taken with each of them has been totally different. It speaks to parenting and how it needs to be different for each child. None of the girls' stories are the same.

There are cohesive components among us; for example, we all dance. We all like making contributions to the world overall. We all have a nurturing compassion to help people heal. I know that they were brought into my life for a reason. There is a strong relevance of my being placed in their existence and them being placed in mine. I know honestly in some of my times of struggle, if I didn't reflect on my children and the reason they were present in my life, I may not have made it. Sometimes my love for them was greater than my strength. They gave me a reason to get through the experience.

To me, fatherhood is about being a leader, teacher, provider, role model, motivator and providing a strong foundation. These daughters have all grown into amazing young ladies. I think they would say there's a part I have played in their lives and where they are.

"Leading by example, Pepper, as my dad, taught me first the importance of how to be a complete human being. He demonstrates maximizing potential, mapping out your destiny by having vision and setting goals, and not to settle for less than your greatest potential," says Corina.

"Over twenty years ago," Mary Wright confides, "when I adopted Kenna from Ethiopia as a one-year-old, Pepper stepped in and took on the father role, even though legally we had no family connection. Kenna refers to Pepper as her father, and we truly are a family, just not in the traditional, legal sense. Pepper takes his part as a role model very seriously. I didn't ask him to be a father to Kenna, and I didn't expect him to do that. It just happened. Being from Ethiopia, I wanted her to have a good, black role model, so I'll always be grateful for Pepper."

Recently, Kenna wrote me a note, saying she was thankful for my constantly working to stay close in our relationship and having long talks with her.

My own dad was raised in a household by his mother and grandmother without the presence of his father. There are certain components of that cycle that have carried over in my life and in my daughter Gabby's life. I may not have been present under the roof during

Gabby's rearing, but you never found a more active and present cheer dad, soccer dad, school dad, parent dad—I was there. Gabby shared with me that she gets the same calm and patience from me that I got from my dad.

CHAPTER 11

Today and Tomorrow

LIFE is not always perfect from our perspective. We will not always get what we want. However, that which has thrown us off course will always bring us back to where it is we need to be. The challenges are what keep me going day to day, even though, at times, these same challenges have nearly crushed me.

Recently, there was a phase where I was living in more fear than faith—a place where things seemed almost too dark and too deep to crawl out of to the light. This starts to manifest itself physically. That's the tag-team relationship the mind has with the body in depression. Your mind says, "I can get you through portions of this, but if you can't pull it together, then I'll send it to your body. If your body can't hold it together, that will cause physical dis-ease."

Depression was taking me down. I felt like I didn't have control, yet I should have. I knew it was depression because I'd been through it before, and I wanted to step out and get help. I made a doctor's appointment. The recommendation was to join a talk therapy group, and for me, that didn't feel safe. The other things conventional medicine had to offer were psychotropic drugs. I knew they weren't the answer for me either. I felt like that hamster running in a cage. I was once again at the point where depression threatened to take over my life and clouded my perceptions and decisions. Somehow, I continued to function, even if it wasn't at my highest level.

FIERCE FUNk®

FIERCE FUNk is my creation. It was developed over years. It is a new, exciting dance fitness program, combining street-style funk movement with a contemporary hip-hop feel for an inspiring, fun and complete workout. The FIERCE FUNk culture is not just fitness and dance; it is a moving energy intended to refresh the spirit so participants are more healthy and happy. My vision is for instructors to bring a sense of fun, empowerment, passion, energy and a philosophy of love toward others in their classes through dance and fitness movements set to energizing music.

FIERCE FUNk has several dimensions. There are different sub-sections—one for teens, one for adults, a workout clothing line and Pepperisms.

Funk used to be called "soul." For me, it goes back to gospel music. Funk is a rhythmic pattern, syncopation, and a feeling you get in your heart and soul that makes you want to cut loose. In funk you move with the flow and at the same time, you've got to be able to isolate your movements with a syncopated rhythm. I tried to explain this to my dance troupes, and some of them couldn't understand what I meant, so I took them to a gospel church, and after that experience, everyone knew exactly what I was talking about.

Music is around us all the time. FUNk works with all kinds of music—contempo funk, rap, pop, be-bop, up-beat jazz, big band and country.

One of the program philosophies of FIERCE FUNk, taken from my civil rights days, is that the goal is bigger than the struggle. I know that whatever I've gone through, my destiny for being born is bigger than my struggles. I can look back on my experiences and ask, "Why didn't I go through with a certain action? Who guided me through the pain and contemplated action in another direction?"

PENDING IMPLOSION

IT was a very scary time. I invested so much into the FIERCE FUNk program, and I knew that it was going to implode. I wasn't quite sure what the outcome was going to be for me or the other people involved. It was one of those times in life when you see the bullet coming, yet feel powerless to stop it. So, you say, "Okay I'm going to take the bullet," but I had no idea what that really meant. I was not concerned so much for myself but for the master trainers who had invested in FIERCE FUNk.

I knew that although things seemed to be going okay, they really weren't, and this challenge would come back around if I didn't face it. I wasn't trusting anyone anymore. I found myself making some decisions that I wasn't totally sure about. All I knew was, even though I didn't know where to go from there, I couldn't stay where I was.

On the surface, everything looked fine, but I kept wondering why things weren't working. I knew the company was going to ultimately collapse, and that meant a lot of people who had invested in it were going to be hurt and go down with it. That's a heavy responsibility, and because of my character I said, "I'll figure out a way to save the FIERCE FUNk program and their interests." Even knowing the program was going to implode, my thoughts were that it couldn't get any lower, and it would turn around if I kept going. But I had no idea how far down it could, or would, go.

It wasn't long before things started coming out that I didn't know existed, because it was someone else's job—someone I trusted—to run the business. Now I had to look under the surface, and things were a mess! And what a mess they were. I had wondered why my business wasn't working as I thought it should be. It was such a brilliant concept, and people fell in love with it instantly all over the world. I kept asking myself, "What was the problem? Why is it stuck? Why wasn't it working? Why am I giving, giving, giving, feeding the machine, but nothing ever comes out of the machine to feed me? Why was it wearing me down? What was wrong?"

Things were very intense, and I realized I had to let go of the reins – let go of the illusion that I had control. I gathered all the people I was concerned about letting down and laid the truth on the table. I had to admit there was nothing I could do. There would be no more sports medicine events where thousands of people were used to seeing FIERCE FUNk in its glory. I had to shut down all the instructor training and certification programs even though e-mails were coming in from people every day who wanted to be certified to teach FIERCE FUNk. Initially that was what I wanted—more people to request being certified. That was no longer the case, and I received all these reminders that made me second guess my decision. Did I pull out too soon? Did I make the right decision?

My business advisers explained that this was just another bullet I had to take. I didn't have the luxury of second-guessing myself. I had to make the decision to keep myself from getting sicker, because my style is to make sure everybody else is okay even at the expense of my own self. I was going to keep showing up for class; I was going to keep smiling. Looking from the outside, everything was going to be great, but I was internalizing everything. My advisers reaffirmed that I hadn't pulled out too soon. I could have waited until the point where I was completely broken—I could have had a nervous breakdown or developed some irreversible disease. They gave me credit for taking things as far as I thought I could before making my decision.

To turn away from taking care of FIERCE FUNk at the cost of not taking care of myself was a hard decision. I had invested so much of my life in the program over the years: my health, my sanity, my finances. I put all my energy and resources into it, and now to turn away and say to my backers and trainers it was over was hard. It was up to them now to figure out how they were going to pay their own bills, figure out how to be happy and find joy. Some of the trainers had been there since the beginning. My decisions would affect their life. They had come all the way in and were totally committed.

In my own darkness, I created worse-case scenarios. I told everyone, "Here's what I can do; here's what I can't do. I can't pull FIERCE FUNk along anymore. I don't know what that means in your life, but at this point, you have some decisions to make. If it is to leave by walking away and never coming back, I understand—I will not think any less of you. In your shoes, I can't say I wouldn't do the same thing. Or you can stick around and see how this whole thing evolves or is reborn. Other than what I've laid on the table, if there is any other way I can be of assistance to you, let me know."

The one constant is the objective that brought FIERCE FUNk to life in the first place. Fortunately, I didn't let that die. I didn't compromise the soul of the intent and the heart of the program. Even though there were explosions all around it, this was the one thing that stayed in people's heart and was what they witnessed in their training. In their hearts, what FIERCE FUNk stands for didn't die and that's what carried me through—this was the food I needed in my soul to continue in spite of the moments when I said, "I quit. I can't stay healthy and continue this way." The troupe—the master trainers and investors— came in and said, "Hold on, let's not throw the baby out with the bath water."

In the end, your mind will try to tell you that you've failed when you haven't, as long as you grow through the process. At some point,

I had to look at them and say, "I believe in you more than what I am feeling right now. I am going to trust you, because I have nothing to lose."

I knew they really didn't understand, but they put their faith in me. The commitment in their hearts stayed. And to my surprise, they all continued to stand behind me with their support.

One of the valuable lessons I learned in this experience was, that in expressing my vulnerability honestly, others would support me. This is extremely difficult for a person like me who is used to being the protector. It is harder being the one everyone else looks up to as having it all together—of being the strong one—and to say to them, "You can't depend on me, because I am now more fragile than you." This was hard on my heart and ego.

All I could see was their investment going down the drain. Their time and money was going to be lost. But I found their love for me was bigger than their self-interest. At the end of the day, they all wanted me to be okay, whatever that looked like. They cared for me more as an individual than for their business. This was a tremendous help.

A corporate-based business model is not my area of expertise. I'm into people. I do energy. I do programming and creativity. I can supply that. Dabbling in the business side completely stressed me out and was sucking me dry.

There are now experts who are on board and restructuring the business. They have taken my vision and are totally revamping the business model. One investor said, "For us to effectively build and run this business, we don't need you to run it. We need you to create choreography, to be out in front of people inspiring them. We need you to hug people. We don't need you to do the business elements. We are experts at that."

At that point, I was so beaten down, I was willing to step aside, let go of control, and let these people do what they know is effective in a business model. We created a partnership with a new vision. Once I saw the new vision, I had a choice. I could decide to not trust them, and stay stuck where I was. Or I could trust them and get out of the way, letting them apply their expertise. Now this was not the way I would do it, but I'd seen the outcome of the way I did it—it wasn't working for anyone! They asked if I was okay with changing directions.

"Absolutely! I'm okay not being frustrated and drained anymore," I said.

I work in a very fast-paced business. Even when you're in it and out there, it could happen that what you do becomes quickly passé! I was running just as fast as everyone else and jumping through hurdles to make things work. I operate in a world that is very cynical. Everyone in this business has an agenda. They will throw you under the bus so fast it will make your head spin if they think they can get one inch farther ahead. If I wasn't careful, my faith in the goodness of people would have been destroyed.

Reflecting back, I can see I was being stopped and shown that I was never going to be totally okay with the way things were, because it was not who I am. I needed to get out of the business and be who I am. I have to admit I felt hesitation in trusting the process.

It is difficult moving on because you move into the unknown. Picture a black box in front of you. You can't see what's in the box. There could be winning lottery tickets or scorpions. You don't know. It can be fear or courage that leads when you stick your hand into the box. It takes courage to overcome the fear factor. It takes courage and willingness to live life. Without the willingness to take action, there is no movement.

Focusing on me, not FIERCE FUNk, we restructured the program. I have developed a new, four-hour workshop that focuses on movement to music. It is for the dance educator, but open to everyone. It is designed to take the instructor's knowledge of movement to music to the next level as an educator. This has a fair market value based on my 40 years of experience as a performer and choreographer. This is a different market from the dance fitness world.

We all do what we have to do to get to a certain point. I equate it to being an Olympic diver. For these athletes to get to the high dive springboard and do all the fancy moves they do, they have to climb, step by step, up the ladder all the way to the platform—the springboard for their talents.

I am focusing now on things that will feed my soul. I want to be teaching, I want to be speaking and I want to be educating. That's where my innate talents lie .

I am reminded that, as painful as this journey with FIERCE FUNk was, I must have the faith that coming into a new arena will prove to be successful. After the restructuring, I can be thankful for how the experiences have contributed to not only my growth and development, but to others' as well.

To survive, I had to be able to compartmentalize and reflect on the history of FIERCE FUNk. I had to say to myself, "What nurtured the birth of it was this… What seemed to be its highest peak was this… The transition from mountain peak to valley was this… Stopping the bleeding was this… And the rebirth was this."

Reflection is a universal process. It is not unique to this particular situation. Reflection can be applied to a person's business or personal life, as an open-ended, ongoing process.

I am a very private person, but people need to see the challenges I've gone through to relate to where they are. I haven't been given anything, but I haven't done this alone either. People have come into my life to help me all along the way. I share my experiences to let others know things haven't always been fun or easy, but you do what you need to do every day. You show up in life. You don't lie in bed thinking, "I can't face another day." I've been there, done that; it doesn't feel good, and it doesn't get you anywhere. It would be one thing if you progress by lying around, but life doesn't work that way. Action is the antidote to fear and depression.

All my gifts are on loan to me, just as yours are, and it's our responsibility to share them. My path is far from direct. I have returned to giving more empowerment talks. I spoke to the employees of the California Lottery. I had a meeting with the Denver International Airport group, followed by a three-day leadership workshop for airline personnel. I plan to do more programs like the choreography for the performances in Soul Quest at California State University, Sacramento.

CURRENT PROJECTS

THE University of Nevada, Reno's Northern Nevada International Center is involved with a State Department program called the Mandela Washington Fellowship. This program is the flagship of President Obama's Young African Leaders Initiative. As part of a leadership workshop, I was invited to speak to 30 delegates from various African countries on leadership, and then choreograph and teach a number that was performed for the Obamas at a state dinner in Washington D.C.

Today, my performing life is centered more around choreography. I am involved with Sacramento Black Art of Dance under the direction of Dr. Linda Goodrich. With other choreographers, I explored the movement of the African and African-American culture from its ancestral homeland within the concepts of modern dance.

CHANGE

It's not the strongest species that survives, nor the most intelligent. It's the one that is most adaptable to change."

- Charles Darwin

CHANGE is the only constant guaranteed in the universe. Fortunately, we have the tools to change ourselves and contribute to change in others. Putting our thoughts into action creates change.

THE LIFE OF THE BUTTERFLY: A STUDY IN TRANSFORMATION

THE life of the butterfly is nature's example of change or transformation. In its life from egg to adult, butterflies undergo a series of physical transformations. After mating, the female butterfly lays her eggs on a specific plant. The egg hatches when the conditions are right, and the caterpillar begins to eat the host plant. During this stage, the caterpillar discards its skin several times as it grows. It then suspends itself by silken threads and sheds its outer layer one last time to become skin that will harden and form the chrysalis. Within the darkness of the cocoon, a metamorphosis takes place creating wings. Struggling makes the wings strong. In the next phase as a fully developed, brightly colored winged adult, the butterfly struggles out of the darkness it created into the light, finally releasing its full beauty. Shortly, it flutters its wings to dry them and flies to freedom. This is the natural progression of its development. Every step is important and leads to the next. And the process repeats itself for every new butterfly. Is this not the story of our own lives?

If the cycle of the butterfly is interrupted there can be disastrous results. One day in the spring, a young boy is walking to school. Along the way, he spies a butterfly struggling to get out of the cocoon. Out of compassion and with the best of intentions, he decides to help the butterfly. Unfortunately, the butterfly's wings are not fully developed and ready for flight. The butterfly falls helplessly to the ground where a cat pounces on it and eats it!

The moral of the story is simply that we can actually love something to death. We all need to work through our challenges to be healthy and grow at our own pace. That isn't to say we don't need help, because we do. As John Donne said, "No man is an island." But before jumping in and helping people, we need to step back a moment and evaluate whether we would be nurturing them, or encouraging them to change prematurely, or enabling them not to change at all.

There is a fine line between nurturing and enabling. When I have said the same thing to a person three times without seeing a change, I know I am enabling. This is not a judgment on my part as to whether or not their actions are ineffective, so much as distinguishing that my actions, like the boy's, are not really helping, even though I would like to help.

Change our thoughts: change the world. Change our actions: change the world. Change ourselves and the world around us will change. As Gandhi said, "Be the change you want to see in the world." We do this by nurturing ourselves and others.

CHOICE IS CHOICE

EVERYTHING in our life is a reflection of a choice we have made. If we want a different result, we must make a different choice.

The final freedom that comes before consequence is the free will to choose what our action will be. Free will is the trigger for change to take place. Free will, or free choice, is the potential for us to experience a variety of lessons and make alternate decisions. There are many options open to all of us at any time; the possibilities are limited only by our vision. Making choices is our contribution to our own destiny. Before examining choice, let's answer the question, "What is Life?"

It is said Life boils down to getting from point B to point D—from Birth to Death—but what's between B and D? It's the letter C. The Cs of life are: choices, courage, confidence and change. We must make the choice to choose the opportunities for change before us, facing them with courage and confidence, or our life will stagnate. Life is therefore a matter of choices.

In the past, the choices made by others have created our present world. And the choices we make create the future. Our choices and actions don't just impact or affect our own immediate life. We can view our choices as the concentric circles we see when a pebble is dropped in still water. Our choices radiate out and go on farther than the eye can see.

In my upbringing, I've been taught that our choices and decisions impact seven generations after us and are the result of the choices made by seven generations before us. A generation is roughly 30 years, so we are talking about our decisions and actions impacting 210 years! We are living now through the choices and decisions of those that were made around 1806, near the founding of our nation. In turn, the legacy we are building right now is not only impacting our own life, but will be carried into the year 2226!

We live in the present, but we have to live and think in broader terms. What our ancestors accomplished now allows us to have the life we have today. Yet, we tend to think in two generations, not looking further than the past of our parents and grandparents or the future of our children and grandchildren. We think about how what we are doing today will impact our children's opportunity to make a living, go to school and raise a family. In thinking about the next generation or two, we should realize how generations after that also depend on what we do today. What we do is critical for the next seven generations. That is our legacy!

My wise grandmother said, "If you're gonna get what you've never gotten, you gotta do what you've never done." That means making the choice to change. Attitude and character play into being a sound human being. What influences our thoughts feeds our desires, dictates our choices, influences our actions, becomes our habits, determines our character and paints our destiny and the future, for seven generations.

CONFIDENCE AND THE PLACEBO EFFECT

CONFIDENCE is faith in the ability to do anything we set our mind to do. Our mind can't tell the difference between what is real and what is not. Having confidence is like the placebo effect. In clinical trials, an inactive substance with no known effect—a placebo—is given to some subjects while others receive the real drug in order to determine the effectiveness of the drug. The minds of the subjects given the placebo can't tell the difference. As a result of the subject's perception, their mind reacts as though they were given the drug. Our minds work the same way. They will believe what our perception is. We will manifest what we set our mind on, and taking it a step further, put it into action. This is often referred to as "fake it until you make it." We're doing that all the time due to the placebo effect. Let's use the power of placebo to concentrate on confidence, success, peace, love, health and happiness.

THOUGHTS AND CONSCIOUSNESS

THE only person we have control over is ourselves. In turn, the one thing we can control, or learn to control through self-discipline, is our thoughts. Though unseen, our thoughts are concrete. This is another reason why the concept of "fake it until you make it," or affirmations, works.

Thoughts also create our consciousness and our future. What we continually and consistently think about, we build. Our consciousness is like constructing a building; one thought equals one hammered nail. The true essence of us as human beings does not lie in our outer shell, but in our inner being—in our thoughts.

The connection between mind and body is through our thoughts. The body's responses to the body-mind connection shift from moment to moment, depending on what our thoughts are and the emotions attached to them. Thus, where our intention goes, our power flows.

One caveat: we need to be careful what we allow to influence our thoughts. Our thoughts are the threads in the fabric we call our life. Before there is fabric, there are threads (thoughts) to be woven. The old adage of being careful what you ask for because you may get it is appropriate.

Consciousness is the awareness of the information and thoughts our brain uses to plot our journey, which creates our reality. Likewise, our consciousness stands behind our thoughts, while our hands have the task of carrying out the duties of our thoughts. With practice, we can learn to control our thoughts. Exercising this kind of control brings peace of mind for whatever life throws at us, and makes our life more effective.

Our purpose is to learn to live productively with our gifts and talents, and to be at peace with the way our world operates today. This starts internally with our thoughts and radiates outward into our actions. Long ago in church I heard, "You are not of this crazy world; you have to learn how to function in this crazy world." That's the lesson.

OUR ACTIONS

ACTION is the enemy of fear and stagnation. However, we must be careful not to confuse action with movement. With action, there is achievement of a goal. With movement, we could just be spinning our wheels and not going anywhere. This is like a hamster in a cage, running on a wheel, expending two valuable resources—time and energy, running until exhaustion but not going any place. Action, on the other hand, brings with it the opportunity for growth.

"Opportunity is missed by most people, because it is dressed in overalls and looks like work," said Thomas Edison. We may never know what results come of our actions, but if we do nothing, there will be no results. It is in our hands to make a better world for all who live in it now and in the future. We cannot settle for a life that is less than the one we are capable of living in joy.

We also must examine all our actions in the light of what the cost will be. I can say I am going to be successful, but at what cost? I can say I'm going to create, but at what cost? I am going to build a factory to manufacture the widgets I've invented, but at what cost will that be to the environment or to others? Every choice of action has a cost.

For the sake of the world, let us allow what is effective to rise above the ineffective by focusing on the positive. Our actions—or lack of action, which is also an action—either contribute to the solution, allow stagnation or contribute to the problem. Every challenge in our life makes us bitter or better. Every lesson comes to break us or make us. The choice is ours whether we become the victim or victor, and create a better future. What will our legacy for the year 2226 be?

When we act on the growth opportunities that are presented to us, more will come. We can't wait until we think we are ready; we are ready when we take action. We just need to have the confidence that we have the power to change our life. And as contradictory as it sounds, sometimes the change we can't change ends up changing us! When we can't change the situation, we can change our attitude about the circumstances.

To change means to be transformed, and transformation is an inside job. Let's go inside ourselves and allow our inside to show on the outside. We shouldn't be afraid of change. Yet, one reason people resist making the choice to change is because they focus on what they have to give up, instead of what they have to gain. We may lose something, but we may gain something better. Just ask the butterfly.

A FEW PARTING WORDS

IT'S amazing how acts of kindness return to us, to be our own incentive and our own encouragement, as we pursue our goals and dreams.

When we give value to the world from our heart, the benefit comes back to us. Paying it forward has its own rewards, even if it happens indirectly or takes years to occur.

What do we say to those people who express how we've touched their life? Touching people's lives is a two-way street. They have given us the opportunity to give, and we have given them the opportunity to receive. A simple "thank you" is enough as we strive to pay it forward again.

The real treasures of life are the way we live and the gifts we give. We don't know how we touch people's lives. I am more and more humbly grateful every time I receive such a message, because it is confirmation Spirit is working through me.

We begin our life as an open book full of blank pages. We write our story as we go. We can't start the next chapter of our life if we keep re-reading the last one. We are not given a good life or a bad life. We are given life, and it's up to us to make an effective life for ourselves and for the benefit of others. Each challenge in our life has shaped us into the person we are today. Let's be grateful for our teachers, the experiences, and the opportunity to change. We have the power to say, "This is not how my story will end," and to make changes.

We need to make sure that our use of power is to spiritualize our life and world. Seek the practical life, but seek it in such a way that does not blind us to Spirit working within. It is not out of spiritual greed that we seek Spirit; it is so we may apply Spirit in our daily life to maximize our greatest potential. Then, we can go out in the world and achieve our highest purpose of serving with love.

In the final analysis, life is not about finding ourselves. Life is about creating ourselves. Let's find the courage to move forward and fulfill our greatest responsibility, which is to maximize our highest potential—physically, mentally, emotionally and spiritually.

Our entire experience is about finding success in the journey. Not knowing what the final result might look like, we live each moment taking full advantage of the opportunity to embrace the process to Live, Love and Laugh. We can learn to choose HAPPINESS (acceptance, gratitude, compassion, joy, forgiveness and peace) even in the face of challenge, change, uncertainty or disappointment. Hopefully, we learn that guilt, upset, self-sabotage, ego, jealousy, envy or any form of emotional suffering is a choice. HAPPINESS is an alternate choice and always available.

My hope is that this work not only inspires and motivates you, but empowers you to choose physical, mental, spiritual and emotional health and happiness.

The world is better for you being in it. Go out and don't miss the opportunity to create a miracle in someone's life today.

CPSIA information can be obtained
at www.ICGtesting.com
Printed in the USA
FSOW02n0939230517
34511FS